ATTEMPTING NORMAL

ATTEMPTING NORMAL

★ Marc Maron ★

SPIEGEL & GRAU

NEW YORK

2014 Spiegel & Grau Trade Paperback Edition

Published in the United States by Spiegel & Grau, an imprint of Random House,
a division of Random House LLC, a Penguin Random House Company, New York.

SPIEGEL & GRAU and the HOUSE colophon are registered
trademarks of Random House LLC.

Originally published in hardcover in the United States by Spiegel & Grau,
an imprint of Random House, a division of Random House LLC, in 2013.

Library of Congress Cataloging-In-Publication Data
Maron, Marc.
Attempting normal / Marc Maron.
pages cm.
ISBN 978-0-8129-8278-7
eBook ISBN 978-0-679-64413-2
Maron, Marc. 2. Comedians—United States—Biography. I. Title
PN2287.M515A3 2013
792.702'8092—dc23
[B] 2013000537

Printed in the United States of America on acid-free paper

www.spiegelandgrau.com

2   4   6   8   9   7   5   3   1

Book design by Christopher M. Zucker

For everyone who is successfully defying their wiring

"Once upon a time called now."

LOLLYPOP MAN,
AKA THE LONG HAIRED SUCKER

Contents

Introduction: The Garage

The garage is a single-car garage that hangs precariously over the edge of a hill in my backyard. When I got the place it had a crumbling cement floor and an old, tool-scarred workbench built into the side. There were holes, cracks, random nails, hammered-in rubber pads, the ghosts of anvils and clamps. A hard man had sweated over engines and machines here, I thought. I put a floor in over the cement and kept the bench as an homage to real work. I put my printer on it.

I always wanted it to be a work space. That was the plan when I bought the house. I think I was hoping it would turn into one of its own volition. But it took a couple of years, a divorce, and profound desperation before the garage became an office rather than just a place where I stored everything I have held on to all of my life.

Before hoarding became a phenomenon, people just called it "collecting" or "being nostalgic." I don't hoard, exactly, but I get it. It's a response to our need and desire for purpose, order, defini-

tion, and a fortress. It's a calling that requires constant manage-
ment, control, and obsessive attention. I am amassing artifacts
from the history of me. My garage is the storeroom and temporary exhibition hall of the yet-to-be-built museum documenting
the rise and fall of the Marc Age. I am the curator. I decide the
meaning and worth of the collection based on my feelings in a
moment. Where does this particular artifact take me now? How
do I contextualize this laminated all-access talent pass from the
1995 Aspen comedy festival?

There are hundreds of books here. I am surrounded by an em-
pire of unread and partially read books. Titles like: *The Denial of
Death* (read), *A Thousand Plateaus* (God, I tried), *The Family*
(Manson phase), *The Hero with a Thousand Faces* (skimmed
hard), *Gravity's Rainbow* (nope), and *The Illuminatus! Trilogy* (of
course). There are several bibles, *The Aeneid, The Odyssey, The
Anthology of American Poetry*. I have Freud, Reich, Barthes,
Fromm, Spinoza, Plato, Hunter S., DeLillo, Bangs, Benjamin,
graphic novels, *Hellblazer* comics, beat poetry, cookbooks.

I am not bragging. I am embarrassed. Most of the books I have
are indicators of my insecurity. I really wanted to be an intellec-
tual. I really wanted to understand Sartre. I thought that was what
made people smart. I have tried to read *Being and Nothingness* no
fewer than twenty times in my life. I really thought that every
answer had to be in that book. Maybe it is. The truth is, I can't
read anything with any distance. Every book is a self-help book to
me. Just having them makes me feel better. I underline profusely
but I don't retain much. Reading is like a drug. When I am reading from these books it feels like I am thinking what is being read,
and that gives me a rush. That is enough. I glean what I can. I
finish some of the unfinished thoughts lingering around in my
head by adding the thoughts of geniuses and I build from there.
There are bookmarks in most of the denser tomes at around page

20 to 40 because that was where I said, "I get it." Then I put them back on the shelf.

There is a box full of hundreds of Polaroids. They were important in the eighties. They were art. Hockney and Warhol made them important. I was an important artist in my teens! I needed to take handheld Polaroids of myself at different phases of my life looking head-on into the camera. Different shirts, facial hair mistakes, hair ridiculousness, silly eyeglass frames, all changing over the years. Some surface manipulation. Smeared emulsion. Art. My head, documented and boxed.

There are hundreds of audiocassettes and videocassettes. Me on *An Evening at the Improv* in 1989, *Caroline's Comedy Hour*, static shots of club sets in different cities, cassettes of sets from more than twenty years from gigs all over the country. I intended to listen to them to learn, to craft, but I didn't really. Documented. Boxed. I lived. I talked into microphones in front of people in a lot of places over a lot of years.

There are two shelves of records. Some I have been holding on to since high school.

Notebooks. There are dozens of notebooks. I always carry notebooks with me. I scribble in them in a barely readable scrawl. I do not write jokes. I write moments. Thoughts. Fragments that I have to sweat over as if they're cryptic texts in a lost language when I try to interpret them. That shouldn't be part of my process—decoding my own writing—but it has been for my entire life. What does that say about me? Why can't I make it easy? I need to complicate everything to protect myself from success and to remain complicated and overwhelmed.

I like to get things framed and to put things in small frames. On the wall: black-and-white photo of Muddy Waters, *Apocalypse Now* lobby card of Dennis Hopper, another of the cast of *Freaks*. A color photo of me and Sam Kinison; a caricature and clipping from the *New Yorker* review of my show *The Jerusalem Syndrome;* the cover of an antidrug pamphlet showing a skull wearing a crown holding a syringe with the words KING HEROIN over it; the poster for my HBO *Half-hour* from 1995, featuring all the comics in the series; my likeness from the Dr. Katz cartoon; three strips from a photo booth with my first real girlfriend; a picture of my ex-wife before she was my wife, before I ruined it; a photo of me and my brother on the day of his wedding, him in a tux, me in a towel; me and my grandfather (I am wearing a Killing Joke shirt); Lenny Bruce dead and alive; the head of St. Catherine; a laminated copy of the *New York Times* article about my podcast; my father at age twenty-five; Frank Kozik's poster for *Gimme Shelter*; Chuck Berry; a *TV Guide* crossword puzzle from 1992 with me as one of the clues: "Host of *Short Attention Span Theater*? MARON."

Why am I holding on to this stuff? Some of this junk is losing its punch. Pictures. Pieces of paper with writing on them—I can no longer connect with the thoughts or feelings that birthed them, that drove me in that panicky desperate moment to scribble in a barely legible scrawl as if on a cave wall. All say the same thing in some form or another: "I am here. This is me in this moment." Do I have some fantasy that this stuff will be important after I die? Do I think that scholars will be thrilled that I left such a disorganized treasure trove of creative evidence of me? Will the archives be fought over by college libraries?

What will probably happen is my brother will come out with my mother and look in the boxes. My mother will hold up a VHS or a cassette and say to my brother, "Do I have a machine that plays these?" My brother will shake his head no and they will throw it all away.

Now the only items that have immediate meaning in my garage are a new table situated in the center of the room and the microphones that are attached to it. Me sitting at that table across from people talking to them on those microphones has changed the trajectory of my life completely.

When I returned from New York City after my last stint at Air America Radio I had already done the first several podcasts. We called the show *WTF* because that was the angle, that seemed to be the most important question to me. I asked a fellow podcaster, Jesse Thorn, what mics I needed. He told me Shure SM7 mics are the mics he uses. I ordered a couple. He showed me how to use GarageBand on my Mac and that was that. A dude I knew who worked at a sound studio brought me some acoustic foam panels he had lying around. There were only a few and I put them up randomly around the garage. One on the ceiling. I have no idea if they even have an effect.

I started asking people to come over and talk to me amid the clutter of my life. People came, hundreds now. The podcast evolved into a one-on-one interview show. I shared many powerful conversations revealing things about the people I was talking to and about myself that I would never have known. Things that will never be said the same way again. It happened organically. I needed to talk and people talked to me. All I am after in the garage is authentic conversation. I don't prep much for interviews. I prepare to talk, to engage, to be emotionally available for an authentic exchange. If I got one of those per episode I'd be happy but I usually get many more than that. Hundreds of thousands of people have joined in on these conversations as listeners, which has affirmed one of the strange beliefs that has shaped my life: People want to share but they usually don't.

People don't talk to each other about real things because they're afraid of how they'll be judged. Or they think other people don't have the capacity to carry the burden of what they have to say. They see the compulsion to put that burden out in the world as a show of weakness. But all that stuff is what makes us human; more than that, it's what makes being human interesting and funny. How we got away from that, I don't know. But fuck that: We're built to deal with shit. We're built to deal with death, disease, failure, struggle, heartbreak, problems. It's what separates us from the animals and why we envy and love animals so much. We're aware of it all and have to process it. The way we each handle being human is where all the good stories, jokes, art, wisdom, revelations, and bullshit come from.

I have met or come in contact with a lot of people over the almost thirty years I've been doing comedy. There are very few people I am not one degree of separation from. I also have a strange heart quirk: I develop oddly deep emotional connections to people in my life that are one-sided. I may be just a passing character to them. I don't know what that is. I don't know why that is. I can have one encounter with somebody and feel connected to them and read a lot into that. They become very important people to me, but to them I may just be like, "Oh yeah, we talked that one time, right?" To me it's a life-changing moment that bonded us; to them, it was a five-minute polite chat in passing. I bring that bond to the talks I have with people. I think if there is any skill to what I do as interviewer it's assuming an intimacy that is probably very one-sided.

That said, it was not like that with Conan O'Brien. I was 165 episodes into my show when he finally said he would do it. I know he is busy. He does a daily show and that is insane, but I really wanted him on. I am very aware of the differences in our lives and work. I have been appearing on his show since 1994, when he was in his first year at *Late Night with Conan O'Brien*. I did standup twice and then wanted to move to panel—the guest on the couch—because I used to love the dynamic between Letterman and his panel guests like Richard Lewis and Jay Leno. I wanted to have that with Conan. He let me, and I have appeared as that guy three or four times a year ever since—except when he hosted *The Tonight Show* that one year, but we are now back at it. I've been on with him upward of forty-five times. What I am trying to say is that Conan and I have a relationship and have since 1994—on camera. We'd never hung out. We never really talked much except a hello in the dressing room and during commercials. Our rapport evolved, but it was always professional. He's been good to me over the years and I always appreciated and was grateful for the times he had me on.

When Conan agreed to come to my garage, it was huge to me. I was nervous. I live in a small house. I was anxious about him judging my life. I felt like I should clean, or move, or build an addition before he got there. I've known him for almost twenty years and he doesn't know my life other than what I tell him on his show. I wanted to make a good impression.

When he came over it was dark out. I opened the door and realized I had never seen him out of makeup or out of the studio. It was bizarre for me. It was a little stilted. He's an awkward guy anyway and he's also very tall. I wasn't sure he would even fit in my house once he walked in. I wanted to get out to the garage as quickly as possible, because I knew in that moment that I had an uncomfortable reverence for Conan. Some part of me felt like I was imposing on this important man who was doing me a favor and we needed to get on with it.

Once we got behind the mics it all flowed very easily. It wasn't about what was said, it was the fact that this was the first time I had really talked to him. He told me stuff that wasn't part of his public narrative and I got to know him a bit. It was emotional for me, because I had always wanted to be his pal in some way, and even more so because he was doing the podcast and that meant I was doing something relevant. I felt proud. I wanted to do a good job because I respected him and in some way it was a turning of the tables.

When we finished we went back into the house and Conan was just sort of lingering. He was looking at stuff on my table, on my walls, and it was awkward again. Not in a bad way, but we were both back to our roles. I was a guy whom he let appear on his show and had a good television rapport with, and he was a star who, in my mind, had better things to do. That might not have been the case. We have a history and we had just had this great talk and now I knew I couldn't say, "Okay, we'll talk tomorrow." Or "Let me know when you want me to come by the house for dinner." Or anything real friends say to each other. It literally got to the point where I was wondering how to get him out of my house because I didn't know what do say or do. It was time for him to go back to his life and me to get on with mine.

But what was important about that situation was that I felt like Conan and I met as equals. I didn't feel small. And it's because I was doing the thing I needed to do. In our interview, Conan said something about the secret of his success: "Get yourself in a situation where you have no choice." And that's what I'm doing, because I had no choice. I was broke and broken and lost when I started *WTF*. I didn't plan it this way. I would've done it the other way if it had happened or I had been allowed to, but it didn't and I haven't. In retrospect I'm not even sure I could have. So I'm stuck with me and that's okay, most of time. That struggle is what I put out into the world.

This is who I am: I overthink and I ruminate. I'm obsessive. But what I really want is relief. Most people are the same. We're all carrying around some shit. When you hear the things that people have gone through and realize you've gone through the same, it provides an amazing amount of relief. It gives us hope. And I think that's what we're supposed to get from each other. The hope that, maybe, just maybe, we're going to be okay. Maybe.

★ Part 1 ★

ATTEMPTING

WTF #111

October 4, 2010

Louis C.K.: The first time I saw you was at Catch, and, um . . .

Marc: In Boston.

L: In Boston, yeah.

M: But, like, you didn't know me, I didn't know you then. But I remember . . .

L: I didn't know you, and I didn't like you on stage the first time I saw you. You were very aggressive.

M: Yeah.

L: And you were also very . . . You were in a lot of turmoil. I think you were just coming out of all this sort of Sam Kinison coke business.

M: Yeah, yeah, yeah, yeah.

L: So you were very . . . You exuded a huge amount of insecurity and craziness.

M: [*Laughing*] Undisciplined, though. Like, I didn't think I was.

L: Yeah, like, you made me uncomfortable. And then I met you . . . And then David Cross, I think, said, "Um, I'm going to hang out with this guy. You wanna come with me?" And he told me it was you, and I was like, "Oh, that guy." So then we went to the Coffee Connection.

M: Where I worked.

L: Where you were working, which is now, like, Starbucks. And you were washing dishes. It was like a movie, like a bad movie. It was like a pile of cups and saucers and you were washing them with, like, a big hang-over-the-sink spigot.

M: Yeah, yeah.

L: And you had an apron on and you were miserable. You were really working hard, and it was a very humbling moment in your life. And you were like, "Oh, you guys, I've got a break in a few minutes, so, you wanna hang out?" And I immediately liked you. Because, that humbling moment made me like you a lot. And it was interesting to then watch you go from being the kinda L.A., long hair, Kinison-pack, coked-up kinda guy. I watched you break that down. And I watched you start talking about who you were, instead of doing your bits as that guy.

M: Yeah, yeah.

L: I started watching you humiliate yourself more on stage, which is a good thing. I mean that in a good way.

M: Yeah.

L: You had a huge humility wave that started coming. I've always [thought] that your progress [came from] taking away more and more layers. Taking more of your defenses away from yourself.

M: Not without a fight.

L: No! But the fight is fun to watch.

1

The Situation in My Head

I had a bad run-in with myself on a plane recently. I had just flown from Dublin to Chicago and hadn't slept much. I was strung out. Tired. Tweaky. I changed planes in Chicago to fly to Los Angeles. Things were vibrating and I was edgy. I was in the exhaustion zone, feeling the kind of tired you can't sleep off because you can't sleep, because your blood is pumping caffeinated dread and loathing.

I was seated at the front of coach in an aisle seat, directly behind the first-class dividing wall and the flight attendant service area. It's my favorite seat on a plane. I like watching people get on the plane so I can judge them. I like judging. I didn't see any real problems among the passengers who awkwardly clumped onto the plane, but I definitely felt like I was in a better place than some of them, which helped take the edge off my mood. Judging works.

We took off. The flight attendants were strapped in almost directly in front of me, facing me. I always scan their faces for fear. I rarely see it. When I do see something dark flicker across their faces, it usually seems like it has nothing to do with the job. More likely something personal that followed them onto the plane. But then again, what do I know. I project. Then I judge.

The crew seemed pleasant. One woman in particular seemed genuinely nice: blond hair, about fifty, pretty in the classic California way. I always wonder when I see older flight attendants if they've been at it since the seventies, when things were crazy. Did she ever have sex in a cockpit? Did she survive a crash? Get tied up in a hijacking? Did she ever have sex in a bathroom with a passenger? With the pilot? I like to give my flight attendants a bit of backstory. I decided she was an out-of-control instigator of major in-flight mayhem back in the day. She got through it disease-free and didn't end up in rehab. She started a family, her husband had a drug problem he couldn't kick and left her, but she did all right. The husband had a lot of money, so she's good. Humble and wise. She lives in Topanga with a few big dogs. Her kids are in college. Only a few people know her from her old life and one of them is the pilot on the flight I am on. That's who I made the flight attendant up to be.

Once we were up in the air I was crawling out of my skin. I couldn't sleep and had definitely had enough of flying. I needed to walk around and judge. I walked down the aisle toward the back of the plane in hopes of going to the bathroom. I didn't really have to go but sometimes it's just nice to lock yourself in the bathroom of a plane and take a few minutes to look in the mirror. I reached the door of the bathroom and the little lock indicator said *Vacant*, but there was a man standing in front of the door. Hanging out, I guess. He was a Middle Eastern–looking man, olive-skinned with Semitic features—a dubious shade of brown. I looked at him and gave him a raised-eyebrow grunt, asking if he was waiting. He looked me right in the eye but didn't speak for a moment. Then he shook his head no. It was a simple gesture, but seemed ominous and cryptic. I couldn't understand why he was standing there. In retrospect he was probably just doing what I was doing. Stretching, moving around. But in that moment, when I looked into his eyes, fear shot through me. I was sure that this guy was up to something. He had that look in his eye. Scheming, driven, full of will and sacrifice. He was clearly Palestinian or Saudi and we were all in trouble. The worst of it was that I was sure I was the only one on the plane who knew that something truly awful was about to happen. I knew and he knew I knew. I could see it in that quick glance he shot me letting me know that he wasn't going into the bathroom. No, he was going into the cockpit. It was that kind of look.

I didn't go into the bathroom. I lingered around in the rear flight attendant station thinking, watching, figuring out what had to be done. The suspicious-looking, dubious-shade-of-brown man started making his way down the aisle. I decided to follow him. I found out very quickly that it's hard to discreetly follow someone on an aircraft. I gave him about ten steps, then I started pacing behind him down the aisle toward the front of the plane. He walked right through the division between the classes, from coach into business. I stopped in the service area, afraid to cross the class line, and watched him disappear behind the curtain. I was completely panicked. I knew he was heading for the cockpit. I hadn't figured out what his plan was but I knew we were all in trouble and no else knew. I had to save us. I pulled the curtain back and focused intently on the man moving toward the front of the plane. I can only imagine what my face looked like or what kind of panic vibrations were peeling off me as I stood there try-ing to figure out a plan, my brain working the angles.

"Is everything okay, sir?"

It was the flight attendant, the one who'd been through some shit and come out on the other side. I turned. She looked concerned. Some part of me knew I couldn't spill everything, that she wouldn't understand if I just babbled out everything I knew. So this came out of my mouth:

"Uh, well, there's . . . a situation. In my head."

"Maybe you should sit down, sir," she said, concerned, like I was the one with a problem.

"Um. I think we . . . okay. Yeah, okay," I said, letting go of my horrible knowledge and the impending crisis for a moment. "I'll sit down. But . . . okay."

I sat down in my seat, my brain still feverishly running scenarios. I knew what was happening. I saw it in my mind. The dubious-shaded-brown man was already in the cockpit. He had on a pair of rubber gloves that had been soaked in an ancient toxin that he had achieved immunity to by exposing himself to it in small doses over the last year. He had already touched the neck of the pilot and copilot, who were in full cardiac arrest with a pinkish white foam coming out of their mouths as they gasped and writhed in their final throes. The man was moments away from taking control of the plane, plummeting us to a lower altitude, and putting us on a flight path into the target of his choice.

I don't make pretty pictures. Sometimes I wish my imagination were fueled by something other than panic and dread. But I don't have control over my gift. It has control over me and I am dragged by it more often than not, away from the idyllic land of normal and onto the jagged shores of self-destruction. Imagining the worst has always been a great comfort to me. If there is turbulence there is an imminent crash. If she doesn't pick up the phone, she is fucking someone. If there is a lump it is a tumor. By thinking like this I protect myself from disappointment. And if anything other than the worst-case scenario unfolds, what a pleasant surprise! The problem is that I am always walking around preparing for and reacting to the horrors of what my brain is making up, living as if every potential terror and every defeat were already happening—because in my mind, it always is. I think if I could just create a series of characters to enact all the heinous possibilities my brain manufactures to insulate me from joy, then I would be using my creativity in a safer way. I see maybe an animated series or perhaps several epic paintings, large canvases. I'm talking the whole wall of the gallery big.

I don't like animation and I'm not a painter. All I can do is imagine these horrors and share them with you.

I sat in my seat powerless, waiting for the plunge. I was squinting hard and clutching the armrests when I felt a tap on my shoulder. I opened my eyes to see the entire flight crew standing over me. The one who seemed to be the leader, a hard-looking woman, asked, "Are you all right, sir? Do you need medical attention?" The kind flight attendant had betrayed me and now stood behind the monster in an apron who was interrogating me. I wondered how I became the problem. If they only knew what was about to happen they would be thanking me for being the one person perceptive enough to see it. I was actually hoping that we'd lurch into a sudden descent at that moment. I was hoping that they would all go flying toward the back of the plane, screaming and thumping along the ceiling. Then they'd know I was right.

I noticed the other passengers were also looking at the problem, which was apparently me. I looked up at the huddled flight attendants, all feigning concern, and I said, "No, I'm good. Thanks."

As this ambush was unfolding I noticed the dubious-shaded-brown man making his way back down the aisle toward an empty seat. His seat. He shot a look at me with those same eyes in which I'd seen a deadly agenda minutes ago. Now they seemed to be smiling and nodding. *Racist.*

"I'm really okay. Just tired. Sorry," I said to the crowd looking down at me. They dispersed, warily. I was embarrassed.

I sat there ashamed. I had profiled. I was delusional. I felt like everyone on the plane was looking at me, the weirdo who freaked out. I sat with my head down the rest of the flight. When I heard the landing gear engage I looked up and saw the flight attendants once again strapping themselves into their little seats. I was a little mad at the ex–wild woman. I thought she'd be cool but she ratted me out. I couldn't hold anyone's eye contact. Just before we touched down she leaned in and asked, "What happened up there?" I looked up at her. She looked caring and sympathetic at that moment. Reluctantly, in a quiet, shaky voice, I said, "I had a situation in my head."

She looked at me nodding and said, "It happens to all of us."

The wheels hit the tarmac.

2

Twenty-Six

Years ago I did a particularly angry set onstage. I talked about AIDS, the end of the world, and how silly and hopeless life was. A guy came up to me after the show and asked, "Why comedy?"

That was all he said. I was dumbfounded.

I started doing comedy in the late eighties. I was raised in Albuquerque, but I went to school in Boston, and that's where my career started, after I placed second in a regional competition sponsored by radio station WBCN. The competition was called the Comedy Riot. There were several rounds; we started out with a five-minute round, then a ten and after that a fifteen. That was probably about all the material I had when I started working, which was immediately after the contest.

Back then there was an unspoken system in comedy. You started at open mics, then you opened or hosted, then you middled or featured, and then you graduated to headlining. Those were the hoops. The time it took to jump through them varied depending on opportunity and talent.

So I started with the open mics. Boston had a few clubs but once I'd run through every one of them, I entered the world of one-nighters, road gigs usually contracted out by bookers to pubs, bars, bowling alleys, hotel conference rooms, dance clubs, VFW halls, college cafeterias, patios, parks, boats, or people's homes—in other words, any type of venue other than one that was conducive to performing comedy. A place called the Boston Comedy Company would book you on a show and you'd go by their headquarters in a basement in Allston and pick up your directions. As an opener I would get anywhere from $50 to $125 to drive anywhere from ten to five hundred miles to open for another act. Most of the gigs were two-man shows. The opener did a half hour and the headliner did forty-five minutes and then you got the fuck out of there unless it was a two-nighter or on an island with no way off, like Nantucket and its Muse, a club that put you up in the "band house," a cinder-block shack out back with bunk beds. There was no choice. There was no boat until the morning. Horrendous.

I drove everywhere to do gigs anywhere: Pancho Villa's in Leominster, Frank's in Franklin, Cranston Bowl in Cranston, Rhode Island, Captain Nick's in Ogunquit, Maine, Jimmy's in Dedham, Nick's at the Kowloon in Saugus, the University of Maine at Machias, the Taunton Regency, Cat on a Hot Tin Roof on Martha's Vineyard, Margaritaville in Worcester. Low ceilings and stale beer and graffiti on the bathroom walls and crowds of angry New Englanders. Among these crowds I felt like a puzzling freak or a crazy but harmless visitor who for some reason demanded everyone's attention all the time. Most of the time I drove home for hours half drunk, chain-smoking in my car and reliving my set. I always felt like I had survived something, that the simple fact that I made it through the show meant I was victorious. But the war wasn't over yet: The next battle was in the car, the war I waged on myself. *I'm not funny enough, that joke didn't work, why can't I stop sweating, fuck those people, I need more jokes, where the fuck am I, shit I don't have a map.* I'll never forget the electricity of postperformance elation and self-flagellation, flying through the New England countryside at night in a VW Golf. Not romantic. But those gigs were my training. I learned to do comedy anywhere for anyone in almost any situation.

One-nighters were contracted out for a certain amount of time and no headliner wanted to do a single minute of material more than necessary, so the opener had to do a full half hour or else get shit from the headliner, who'd be forced to stretch his material to make up the time. If you were opening you were also probably driving the headliner to the gig—so if you didn't do your time, it could be a long ride home.

Around the time I was starting out, a comic named Frankie Bastille had just moved to Boston from Cleveland. He has since passed and I'm not sure that many mourned him. He was a comic gypsy, a road warrior, a drug fiend, and a borderline criminal. I liked him but I was in the minority. One of the first one-nighters I did was with Frankie. We would go on to do several more but the routine was always the same as that first time. I'd go to his apartment building to pick him up. As I was walking down the hall I'd hear a voice screaming down the hallway from behind a closed door somewhere, "Where's my tooth? Where's my fucking tooth?"

That first time I knocked on his door, Frankie opened it and smiled big, revealing a missing front tooth.

"Hey, man. You the opener?"

"Yeah. I'm Marc."

"Frankie. I can't find my tooth."

Frankie had a false front tooth on a mouthpiece that he would always seem to misplace. The ritual of finding the missing tooth repeated itself every time I had to pick Frankie up. More often than not the tooth was very close by, sometimes in his pocket.

He looked ragged in a rock-and-roll kind of way, a bit like Keith Richards, which he was aware and proud of. He had a Tibetan chant tattooed around one of his arms and he was charming like a con man. You wanted to be around him but you didn't want to get too close, leave him alone with your stuff, or owe him anything.

That first gig I worked with Frankie we had to drive a couple of hours into Connecticut to do a show at a bar and dance club. The entire way down Frankie laid down the law. He kept saying, "The most important thing is doing your time." He also recited to me a poem called "The Road," about being a road comic. I can't recall what it was but it was earnest and celebratory, like a pirate shanty.

I was nervous about doing my time. I had not done many gigs and was just getting up to around a half hour. The club was packed. There was a disco ball hanging over the crowd and lots of mirrors around. I took the stage and did all the jokes I had.

When I'd finished my act, I said, "Thank you very much. You're a great crowd. Now, let's welcome your headliner to the stage. He does clubs and colleges all over . . . Frankie Bastille." The crowd cheered but Frankie did not take the stage. The clapping tapered off and I was still standing at the mic. No Frankie in sight. I tried again: "Please welcome, Frankie Bastille . . ." Nothing. The room is starting to get that awkward tension. I am not sure what to do. Then a voice comes out of the darkness, from the back of the room.

"Twenty-six."

It was Frankie.

"What?" I said, panicked, squinting into the darkness.

"You did twenty-six minutes. You have four minutes left."

"Uh . . ."

I scrambled and did a street joke and then brought Frankie up.

He did his forty-five and we got in the car to drive home. I started to apologize but he cut me off.

"You gotta do your time, man," he said, and that was it.

I did not aspire to be Frankie. He was infamous in certain comedy circles but not really respected or liked. No one really knew him and he liked it like that. In the eighties there were a lot of people doing comedy who just seemed to be keeping a few steps ahead of the IRS, ex-wives, and parole officers. Frankie was one of them. There was a story that he was arrested walking off stage for a parole violation and the cops found out because they had heard him on the radio plugging his weekend show. He learned his lesson. From that point on he didn't give out head shots. He didn't want to be on the marquee or in the paper. He didn't stay in any one town very long. He always had people after him for one reason or another.

I figured Frankie liked drugs but I had no idea what he was really up to until we took a trip down to Cape Cod. The gig down there was at a massive Chinese restaurant called Johnny Yee's. The comedy show followed a Polynesian dance show. The restaurant had a huge stage that they pulled out for the dancers and then rolled back in when they were done. The stage that was left for us was six feet high and you had to walk up some stairs to get on it. There was a moat of a dance floor between you and the first row of tables.

It was in Yarmouth, so it was about an hour-and-a-half drive. I picked up Frankie, we looked for his tooth, and hit the road. Once we got onto the Cape Frankie asked me for a dollar bill. I gave him one. He rolled it up. He pulled a small packet out of his pocket. It was a bundle of what looked to be ten smaller packets. I know now these were dime bags. He ripped one open, stuck one end of the bill in the bag and one in his nose, and snorted the contents. He sniffed a bit, looked at me, smiled, and said, "You ever try heroin?"

"No," I said, concerned but curious.

"You want to?"

"Not right now. Maybe later," I said. I was driving a car.

Then Frankie started to nod off. I watched his body drift and sway with the car. He was in and out of consciousness. I stopped for gas and while I was filling up the car he woke up, stumbled into the office of the gas station, and stole a stack of the station's business cards. He started scratching out "Joe's Shell" with a pen and putting his name on there. He thought this was hilarious. I still have one of the cards. When we were about fifteen minutes from the gig he passed out cold. When we got to Johnny Yee's I had to walk him into the club and lay him out in a booth. The guy who booked the place, this three-hundred-pound guy in a Hawaiian shirt named Wayne, asked me if he was okay. I said I thought so but I wasn't sure. I had never dealt with a guy on the deep nod before.

Since I was opening the show I couldn't really keep my eye on Frankie. I got up onstage and did my time, all of it. When I introduced Frankie I wasn't afraid of him shouting out my time. I was afraid of him not coming onstage at all. The last I saw him he was hunched in a booth. I announced his name with a slight inflection at the end—"Frankie Bastille?"—and he bounded onto the stage, took the mic, thanked me, and proceeded to do one of the most engaging, animated live stand-up shows I have ever seen. He worked the stage, he acted out his bits, and he sweated profusely, like no one I had ever seen onstage sweat. He finished and got a standing ovation.

I sat in the booth in the back baffled and amazed. All I could think was *that guy is a fucking pro.*

We got into the car after the show and within seconds Frankie was back on the nod. He stayed that way for the entire trip home.

I didn't want to be Frankie, but I didn't mind being with him, watching him nod off in the car seat next to me after a killer set. That, I thought, is a comic.

The only plan I've ever had in life was to be a comedian. I've never been sure why, but as I get older I'm starting to think it was because I needed to finish the construction of myself. Why I chose comedy for this undertaking is confusing but is starting to make sense to me.

When I was a kid I believed that I wasn't like anyone else. That everyone else knew how to get along and move easily through life. I was alone in a world with no definition, surrounded by the clutter of purpose. My life has been a series of attempts at creating a self that fit somewhere, that engaged easily with others, that people liked or could at least *see*. Something defined. I fed on the acknowledgment, approval, and acceptance of others. Then I resented people for accepting the charade.

I only felt comfortable with people who were missing the same pieces of themselves that I was. I've always been happiest around *characters*. Well-defined and brash personalities. Focused charisma and intensity. Rage. Humor. Flaming self-destructiveness. Missing teeth and tattoos and Baggies in the glove compartment.

The rebels and outlaws, fuckups and con men—comics—had figured it out. They knew the tricks to get by and get life and get what they needed through charm and device, without feeling the pain of not being whole or the injustice of need. They were, like all artists, masters of the mathematics of relief, which was just the sort of thing I was looking for: a book, a movie, a crazy person, a kiss, a drug, a commitment, a song, a phrase, a joke. I thought that shit was magic.

They were my people. And that's why comedy.

3

The First Marriage

I guess we can start at the end but it's really the middle. Let's just call it the really bad part. My second wife, Mishna, brought it to my attention that I had an anger problem. She didn't say it like that. What she said was, "I'm leaving."

Then she took her vagina and left.

I had it coming, I guess. I knew from the start that all I was doing was trying to hold on to her because she gave my life purpose and she was fucking stunning. That's a lot of pressure to put on a person. Maybe if I had just relaxed, trusted myself, trusted her, didn't freak out, everything would have been okay, but I am not capable of doing any of those things. We were fighting the odds from the beginning. When I met her I was a miserable drunk and she was just a kid. I was also married.

My first wife, Kim, was a nice woman. I loved her. I shouldn't have married her. I did it because I didn't know how to break up with her. I was too scared. It was too comfortable. She was a bit naïve. I was a bit out of my mind. I thought that's what marriage was rooted in: fear, comfort, and lies. The triumvirate. I had grown to believe that I would never be happy but if I at least were married I could rest my chaos on a firm emotional mattress, that marriage would make things okay, normal-ish. They weren't. I felt like I was drowning in my bed.

I understood exactly what I was getting into with my first marriage. It was 1995. I was a thirty-two-year-old comic. When I met her, six years before we got married, I was just starting out. Comedians in their infancy are generally selfish, irresponsible, emotionally retarded, morally dubious, substance-addicted animals who live out of boxes and milk crates. They are plagued with feelings of failure and fraudulence. They are prone to fleeting fits of manic grandiosity and are completely dependent on the acceptance and approval of rooms full of strangers, strangers the comedian resents until he feels sufficiently loved and embraced.

Perhaps I am only speaking for myself here.

I was looking for something that would make sense of things. I didn't know what. It was vague to me. I had an itchy soul.

My brother was getting married. He asked me to be the best man. I was all fucked-up on drugs at the time. I go to the wedding and it's a big Jewish event. We're all under the chuppah. My brother's marrying this woman. She's got a hot Jewish maid of honor who is giving me some heat. I'm looking at the bride-to-be through the haze of a cocaine and booze hangover and thinking to myself, "If she's going to take my brother, I'm going to take her friend." That's sort of like love at first sight.

So I charmed her friend, aggressively. Fortunately for me, she lived in the same city, Boston. So within a few weeks, I'd moved my boxes into her apartment and terrorized her into loving me, sweetly. I was the black sheep, the brother failing rehab who had hung his hopes on a dream of show business, and was nothing but fucking trouble. Somehow, she found all of that very appealing. I was her ticket out of middle-class Jeweyness. She was my ticket back in.

I was with her for about six years before I asked her to marry me, which only means one thing: I shouldn't have done it! If you wait six years to get engaged, you are on the fence. I should have known that. I should have known when I bought her a ring and proposed to her in front of the Phoenix airport. She got off a plane, she got in the car, I took out the ring, I said, "So you wanna break up or do this?" I'm paraphrasing, but it was something like that. And she agreed to marry me.

From the minute I got engaged to that woman I knew I shouldn't have done it. I was not stable, I loved her but was not really in love with her, I was not a good man. I was just looking for something that would make me normal; make everything make sense. I figured: bourgeois, middle class, Jews. That should do it. Her dad was a psychiatrist. In retrospect he must not have been a very good one. I mean, he let her marry me. How did he misread the signs so badly? Or maybe I'm that good an actor.

As soon as I put that ring on her finger a switch was thrown. Rooms were being rented, bakers called, invitations sent out; family members were bickering and I might as well have been standing on a dock waving goodbye to a boat sailing off without me. Or maybe my body was on board, dead-eyed and vacant, but my mind was still on the dock, waving.

At first I thought we were going to get married on a mountain at sunset. But there were Jews involved, so that wasn't going to happen. Her mother put the kibosh on that plan with one sentence: "Esther can't make it up the hill." There's always an Esther and she's not going up the hill.

The other switch that got thrown the moment I got engaged was the one in my head that dropped the needle into this groove: *How the fuck did I get into this? Why am I in this? How do I get out of this?* Right up to the day of our wedding I was thinking, "I can't do this."

As I got closer, the fantasy started to take shape: "What if I just walk out on the altar?" That would've been amazing.

Can you imagine if you were up on the altar and the rabbi said, "Do you take this woman?" and you said, "You know what, I don't! HA HA HA!!!" What a cathartic, profound moment that would be. At that moment everyone you know in your life would think you were a fuckin' asshole and you would be truly free. How often do you get that opportunity? "Yeah, fuck all of you!" You could just step out from under the chuppah, walk slowly past a crowd of stunned faces, climb onto a horse, ride to Mexico, and become a cowboy. That's how real cowboys are made. Show up at a bar in Juarez and say, "Hola, amigo. What can I get for this ring?" Clink.

I didn't do that. I married her. I married her for the wrong reason—because it was safe. I believed at that time that people got married when they had that moment, when they're looking at themselves in the mirror and say, "Holy shit. I'm going to compromise my dreams, get fat, sick, old, and die. I kind of want to have someone around for that." You don't want to be sixty, fat, sick, and alone saying to your reflection, "Look at me. I'm a fat failure." No, you kind of want someone around to say, "It's okay, baby. You look great. Let's go get some Tasti D-Lite, cowboy." You're thinking, "I'm not a cowboy. I missed that window. Ah, Mexico."

We were living in Manhattan but when we got married we moved out to Astoria, Queens, to be married people.

Right away I started to bust out. I had a barrel of monkeys on my back. I liked cocaine, I liked pot, I liked drinking. I was trying to keep it all under control. I was married to a woman who wouldn't tolerate it but it started to sneak up on me. I was going on the road hanging out with gypsies and freaks and pirates and

I'd come back all sweaty and broken saying, "I don't know. I think I caught the flu on the plane." It was nuts.

Yes, pirates. Real pirates. I don't know what your experience is, but if you're on a three-day blow bender, you're going to meet a pirate. At some point after you've been up for about seventy-six hours in a strange apartment or hotel room you're going to hear yourself say to someone else in the room, "Dude, why is there a pirate here?" and that person is going to say, "Be cool. He brought the coke." And you're gonna say, "Okay, he's cool, but does the talking parrot have to stay? Because I'm fucked-up, man. It's freaking me out."

"Marc, there's no parrot. You have a drug problem."

"That's what the fucking parrot said! Are you two working together? Why don't you both get the fuck out of here and I'll talk to the pirate for six hours."

I was starting to bring the drugs home. I was not a weekend cocaine user. I'd say I was more like a half-a-week cocaine user. It's amazing how much you can rationalize when you're on drugs. I could actually say to myself, "Look, I'm only doing blow Wednesday through Saturday." I didn't think I had a problem. I thought I was completely under control. I thought, "I have parameters here. I have a schedule. It's Wednesday through Saturday." It took me a long time to realize, "Wednesday through Saturday? You know what, Marc? Regular people *never do coke*! It doesn't even cross their minds." I would get to the drug dealer's house early because I thought if I started early I could be done with it by nine or ten and get on with my day. Like that ever worked. Have you ever heard anyone say, "No, no, I'm good. I've had enough blow. Time to get on with my day"?

One day I got to the coke dealer's house in the late afternoon, before it was dark. I was the Early Bird Special guy. When I got there he was pulling down the shades and then there was a knock on the door. A short old Colombian man with a ponytail walked in. He handed my dealer a wad of tinfoil in exchange for some cash. He was the source. I said, "Let me do some of that!" My dealer said, "Okay, just a line."

He opened the foil to reveal what seemed to be a jewel of blow. He flaked some off the rock into two lines. I snorted them. I felt a tingling behind my eyes that spread up through my brain like a wildfire of joy coursing through my nervous system. Apparently I had never felt the effects of pure cocaine. I said, "Holy shit! Why don't you just sell that?" He said, "Because people would never leave me alone." Then he crushed the gemstone and dumped it into a Baggie of last night's stepped-on crud. It was heartbreaking.

My comedy career was stalled. Dramatically stalled. I was all bloated and sweaty and fucked-up. I was hosting segments on a local TV program on the Metro Channel, which I don't think even exists anymore. It was awful. I would interview people on the street at a desk we would haul around the city. It was a "talk show on the street" segment. It was cute but like being dead but accepting it. I was married to a woman who had just added prenatal vitamins to our kitchen vitamin lineup. I was thinking, "That can't happen."

I'd surrendered. I'd given up. I would lie in bed blasted on coke with my heart exploding out of my chest, next to somebody sleeping comfortably, and I wanted to wake her up to tell her I was dying but I would've rather just died.

I thought that was the only way to get out of my situation. I wanted my heart to explode. I didn't have the guts to leave her. I didn't have the guts to be honest. I was fucked. My career was done. I was bitter.

Then a miracle happened, I guess you can call it a miracle. I'm going to go ahead and call it that even though it ended up the disaster with which I opened this chapter. But at the time it seemed like a miracle, a silver lining. Maybe it was just foil.

I'm at the Comedy Cellar in New York. I'm hanging out. I'm sweating. I'm talking to a few young comics. I'm probably having one of these conversations: "Well, I think if you really want to talk about the history of it, Pryor was really the first. . . ." You know the rap. Holding court. And this woman comes up to me. This woman like a spirit, an apparition. I didn't know who she was. What she was. But this six-foot-tall, spectacular-looking being walks up to me and says, "Hey, you're Marc Maron, aren't you?"

"Yeah. Yeah, I am," I say, defensive but as charming as possible.

"What happened to you? You look like you're going to die."

"Huh? Yeah, well . . . what? I'm cool, I'm good. What do you mean? What's the deal?"

"I'm just a big fan, and I don't know, you look like you're in trouble. If you want to get sober I can help you get sober."

"What? You mean like meetings, AA and that kind of shit? Like the God thing? Are you a God person?"

"I can just point you in that direction."

"Uh, okay," I say.

In my mind I had no desire to get sober or even live, but every part of my mind and body wanted to be as close to her as possible, so I said, "Yeah. Hell yeah, I want to get sober. I need to get sober." But in my mind all I was thinking was, "I'll do anything with you. I'll go anywhere. I'm going to follow you home now even if you don't want me to follow you home." And I did.

We walked thirty-five blocks. I smoked. We talked about cigarettes and about addiction and about comedy and about everything else. We got to her apartment. It was a walk-up on Forty-sixth Street. I'm in her living room smoking a joint, holding a Foster's, and saying, "So, get me sober! Come on. What do you got?"

I start going to meetings, to lunch, to dinner, to wherever this perfect woman wanted to go. I fell in love as much as a newly sober, insane, angry bastard who was miserable and married could be in love, but I was in love, which meant I was going to hang every one of my hopes on this twenty-three-year-old girl. I was thirty-five.

Of course, I was married to another woman. That put a crimp in things a little bit. Courting is difficult when it has to be shrouded in mystery and secret pager codes. There was no texting then, just pagers. So we had numbers that meant, "I love you," "I miss you," "What are you doing?" I was running around the city, sweating and beeping.

Love is love and being in love is being in love. Wherever your loyalty is, whatever rules you think you won't break in your life, sometimes you just can't fight being in love. Some of the best memories of my life are moments like following her up the stairs of that Forty-sixth Street fourth-floor walk-up apartment. Watching her move up the stairs in a plaid skirt, watching her smoking cigarettes, and then laughing on her old couch, lying in her bed after we had sex and listening to her piss, feeling impressed and ecstatic, like, "Holy shit! Listen to that! It's so powerful!" I told my friend Sam about my fascination with the power of her stream and he said it sounded like I was talking about a Thoroughbred horse. I think I was. I thought, "Maybe this is my chance to disrupt my bipolar Jew gene line."

I didn't know what to do. I'm in love with this woman, I'm married to this other woman, and I'm in trouble, so I call my two friends. That's all I need, two. I need the main guy and the guy I go to when I drain the main guy.

The guys at that time were Sam, a bitter and brilliant writer, who was married and had just had a kid, and Dave, a comic and borderline sexual predator. I call Sam first and I say, "Dude, I'm in love. This is crazy. Things have been over with Kim and me for years. What should I do, man? This woman is perfect. I'm getting sober. It's everything I wanted." He says, "Man, you're married. Be responsible. You made a commitment. Try to honor it. This thing will pass." I say, "You know what, man? Take a day off." Then I call Dave. "Hey, Dave! What's going on? Take a break from pursuing eighteen-year-olds online and talk to me. I'm in love with this woman. She's twenty-three and I'm married but I'm getting sober and I think it's the right thing." And Dave, thank God, says, "Ah, dude . . . you gotta go for it! What the fuck, man?! You only live once. This is it! This might be it!" And I'm like, "You're right, man, thanks. I knew I could count on you."

We all have the right to cherry-pick the advice given us in order to do exactly what we wanted to do in the first place.

As I said, courting is a little difficult when you're married and when you're newly sober and when the woman's only twenty-three and you're a dozen years older. I just know that in traditional courting this is not a conversation you should have after sex:

Me [*yelling*]: So, are we doing this, or what? Because I'm going to fucking leave her. Are we doing this? Do you fucking love me? Do you fucking love me? Are you taking me? Are we doing this?

Her [*crying*]: I don't know!

Me [*still yelling*]: What the fuck!? Yes or no? Are we doing this?

Her: I guess so.

Me: Good enough. I'm on it.

If you don't believe in magic, if you don't believe that there are phrases, incantations, mantras, that can change the universe completely, literally change the entire course and trajectory of your life, even the objects in your periphery, you are wrong. There are. This is one of them: "Honey, I'm in love with someone else, and I'm having an affair with her." Abracadabra! Locks are changed. Objects are moved and missing. You are dispatched into exile to a sublet on the Lower East Side, where you will remain alone, isolated, broken off from the world you knew. You deserve it. You have cut yourself off from a wife, a family, a future, your money. Everything.

But I had that girl. Yes. I had that girl. And she was enough.

We embark on this crazy thing, this girl and I. I'm getting sober. I'm going to meetings all the time. I'm writing a book. I'm doing a one-man show. Things are okay. I know some of you are thinking, "What about that other woman, you heartless fuck?" Yeah, what about her? She was a good person, I know. I felt like shit, but I had to do what I had to do. And some of you may think, "Well, you didn't have to do that." Well, yeah, I did. I did have to do that. It saved my life. I divorced that woman and married that girl and she eventually left me. Karma? Sure. She got me sober, though. I am still sober. I have her to thank for that.

I actually use sobriety to try to frame the pain of my second divorce. I was at the Comedy Cellar one night, miserable and in the middle of it. I was talking to the late Greg Giraldo, who was always struggling with drugs and alcohol. A struggle he eventually lost. I asked him how much money he had spent over the years on rehabs. He said, "About two hundred and fifty grand."

My divorce cost me less than that. And I am still sober.

In the middle of my second divorce, from this once-magical woman, I was a broken man. I was fucked-up on all levels. I was on my way to my mother's in Florida, which means I was in real trouble because she is really the last person I ever want to lean on. Not that she's a bad person; she's just a bit boundaryless and draining. I'm at the airport in Los Angeles. I'm walking through the terminal to my gate, trying to catch a 6 A.M. flight. Shattered. My duffel bag was even sad as it bounced off my butt as I walked. I was about four months into my separation from Mishna. I looked up from my drudging and that's when I saw her: Kim and her new husband, standing with their luggage at the gate I was passing.

I think, "I can't handle this. There's no way." So I do that thing where you put your hand up over your forehead, look the other way, and think, "There, I'm invisible."

I know she knows everything. Her best friend is my brother's wife. She has to know all about the disaster that my life's become. I get past the gate and I think I'm out of the woods but then I hear, "Marc!"

I turn around and there's nine years of history running toward me with a very familiar gait. She gets to me and asks, concern in her eyes, "How are you doing?"

I explode in tears and uncontrollable blubbering. I cannot stop it. And without missing a beat, my first wife says, "Not so good, huh?"

I was so happy she had that moment. I deserved it, she deserved it. And the sick thing about me is that right after we had that exchange there was a part of me that thought, "So, are we good? Can I go with you now?"

★ 4 ★

Two Prostitutes

I don't do prostitutes. I am not a hooker guy. I have had two experiences with prostitutes. Neither of them was fun or sexy or hot or anything but disturbing. They happened sometime in the late eighties when I was a struggling comic living in Boston.

I was staying at my girlfriend's apartment near Symphony Hall. The neighborhood was dicey late at night, in a crackhead-and-hooker kind of way. I remember on one occasion I got up to move my car from one side of the street to the other at six-thirty in the morning and this woman walked up to me looking very drug-frazzled and soul-hungry in a very skanked-out and evil way. She grabbed my crotch and said, "Do you want a date, baby?"

It was that kind of neighborhood.

One night I had been out doing a show. Afterward I got all hopped up on blow and booze and made my way home at about three-thirty in the morning. The woman I was living with was out of town. After I parked the car a sketchy-looking guy wearing a fedora walked up to me and said, "Coke?"

"I'm good," I said.

There was a woman walking behind him, short, too much makeup, maybe Latino. She said, "You want a date?"

At that moment, not a rare moment, I was consumed with self-hatred and really high. That is the magical combination that brought me to "yes."

"How much?" I asked. I had never paid for sex in my life.

"Thirty," she said.

So this was not a high-end escort situation. This was a dirty street hooker situation.

"Okay, what do we do?"

"Where's your car?"

"I live right here," I said.

Bringing her into the house that I shared with my girlfriend was like polluting our home with the evil essence of street.

We walked up four flights. She was wheezing after one. "How many more flights?"

"A few more," I said in the middle of my own steep shame as-cension.

We got into the apartment. She was catching her breath.

"What do we do?" I asked like a moron.

"You have the money?"

I handed her thirty dollars. She put it in her purse and started to breathe normally.

"Is this your first time?"

"Paying for it? Yes."

"Well, don't worry, baby. Lie down and take your pants off."

I lay down on the bed. She kneeled between my legs and hunched over me and started giving me head. It was just ugly. It wasn't working for me. There was too much shame, weirdness, and coke so I asked, "Can you take your shirt off or something?"

"It's ten more bucks."

I pulled a ten-spot out of my wallet and handed it her.

"Okay, here's ten dollars."

She took her shirt off and put my hand on her breast and said, "Do you feel a lump in there?"

"Really?"

She continues to go down on me and I'm feeling her breast for lumps. I guess you get what you pay for because it was definitely not sexy and I did feel a lump. It was horrifying. I had a moment where I thought maybe she should be paying me for the examination.

"Uh, yeah, there's something there."

"I know, right? I have to get that checked out."

"Yeah, you should definitely get a second opinion."

She's sucking my cock on and off throughout this exchange. Then the phone rings and it's my girlfriend leaving a message. We hear it in the room. I'm lying there with my cock in the mouth of a woman whose possibly cancerous breast is in my hand, a woman I'm paying to have sex with on our bed, and I hear, "Hi, honey! I guess you're sleeping. Just calling to say I love you and I miss you."

"Is that your girlfriend?"

"Uh, yeah."

"That's nice."

I couldn't have imagined that such a perfect storm of shame and self-hate was possible in one scenario. Somehow I was able to finish because once I set my mind to something I can usually follow through. It was a very sad orgasm. My dick was crying.

When I'm done she of course tells me she doesn't usually do this, that she works with computers. Then she asks if she can take

my cigarettes and condoms from my dresser and all the loose
change. I say sure. I thank her, let her out, and I immediately go
into the bathroom and I scrub myself like I am dirty under my
skin.

I really tried to believe that she worked with computers.

My second hooker story was a similar situation. This one is a little
more poetic. I had moved to Somerville, which was, at the time,
a malignant suburb next to Cambridge, but once again found
myself in downtown Boston. I had just finished a set at Nick's
Comedy Stop. It was two-thirty or three in the morning, the
magic hour, apparently. I was partying with some comics at a bar
that let us stay after closing, just a block from the infamous Com-
bat Zone in Boston, a nasty few blocks of depravity and dirty fun.
I'm in my car, in the Zone, driving home, festering, high, and
hating being me. I see this hooker walking that walk down the
street and I think, "Ugh. All right, I'm going to try again."

I pull up and she gets in the car. I'm coked out of my mind. I
ask her how much and she says thirty dollars. So, again, I'm dealing with a very high level of escort here.

"Thirty bucks for a blowjob?"

"Yeah." She has a bit of grit and gravel in her voice. It is the far
end of the night. Who knows what she has been through already.
How many cars? Cocks? I give her the money.

"Okay, where do we go?" I say nervously, coked.

"Just pull around the corner up ahead." Layered beneath the
rasp in her throat is that undeniable and annoying New England
accent.

So I pull around the corner, park, and ask, "What now?" I am
still not experienced with street hooker etiquette or process.

"Pull down your pants."

I do. She places a condom over my coked, frightened cock,

which, at that moment, is frantically trying to retreat into my body. Rightly so.

"What's wrong?"

"Nothing."

Then she looks at me and says through her phlegm, "I don't usually do this. I'm just in town for my father's funeral."

I think, "Huh?" That is just too deep to take in. Maybe this is her way of grieving. It ripples my mind with sadness.

Just as she is about to start working on me, two squad cars come out of nowhere and surround my car. Their headlights blind me. I panic and say, "What do I do?"

"Well, I think you should pull up your pants. I'll deal with this."

I do what I can in the moment.

She gets out of the car and goes into some shtick with the cops. Talking about how I saved her from her boyfriend who was beating her up. I can't immediately tell if they are buying it.

A cop comes around to my window. I open the window. He shines a light in my face. This is a time in Boston when they list busted johns in the paper. It is not the kind of press I am looking for.

"Where do you live?" the cop asks.

"Somerville."

"Why don't you go there."

"I will. Thanks, officer."

My heart was pounding with cocaine and fear as I drove down the expressway. I was relieved. I couldn't believe he let me off. There was enough coke and alcohol in my system to bust me for DWI, never mind the two lines of blow I usually saved for breakfast in a bindle in my pocket. Once I got out of the Zone and down the road a bit I looked down and saw that I had not really pulled my pants up properly. They were halfway up and my underwear was still down. The head of my dick was sticking out of the top of my pants, with a half-unrolled condom hanging off it.

It was mocking me, reprimanding me. It was angry and disappointed with what I almost put it through, not to mention ashamed.

That was the last time I ever paid for a prostitute. It only cost me seventy bucks to discover that I am not a prostitute guy. And my consolation is that I helped two women: one to confirm her fears and hopefully get to a doctor; the other, apparently, to process the death of her father.

We do what we can.

★ 5 ★

Mother's Day
Card from Dad

My dad sent out this Mother's Day card to my brother's wife. My brother forwarded it to me because we tend to forward each other our dad's brainskids of weirdness in the rare moments when they are documented.

Let me set the scene: It's one of those formatted "fun" emails. It's laid out like a greeting card. It has an owl in the upper left-hand side, sitting on a branch, against a wood-grain backdrop, and it says:

HAPPY MOTHER'S DAY AND

GRANDMOTHER'S DAY CHECKED OUT A FEW QUOTATIONS.

"I used to think it a pity that her mother, rather than she, had not thought of birth control." Muriel Spark

A daily life treating iatrogenic and street-trading drug dependent hard heroin addicts and lackluster unenthusiastic sad specimens of society bring validity to

that quote. Human pollution is the drug world legal
and illegal. Couple that with the industrial pollutants
destroying our food chain, the GEO *(genetically engi-
neered crops) and creatures improving our capitalism
profit margin* add the threat of Muslim domination in
Europe and bawalah(sp) modern society takes on a
beauty all of its own.

My dad is a doctor. I don't even know what *bawalah* means. If
you have forgotten, this is a Mother's Day card.

"The doctor of the future will give no medicine but will
interest his patients in the care of the human body, in
diet, and in the cause and prevention of disease." Thomas
Alva Edison reassures me that my "hobby practice" of
Wellness and Ideal Immunity passed through at least
one genuine genius mind. Have a good and growing following in that area alone. The stumbling block is poverty of the masses making CHO (carbs) the staple of all
diets, severely low vitamin D, inadequate other vitamins, few omega 3s especially during pregnancy-lower
IQ of baby 8–10 points due to impecunious existence
and severe family ignorance. Coupled with wrong social choices and denial that a radio TV news and news-
paper exist, even worldwideweb-only news would be
welcome.

Again, this is a Mother's Day card.

"Thinking out of the box is a learned process that
should be next to godliness in the priorities in what to
teach your children. The trick is to recognize when the
box, itself, is faulty and deserving change." Barry Maron

while watching and hearing a jury of 12 peers in Oklahoma make a decision in a medical malpractice case against a loser doctor. Shades of the OJ jury nullification.

In case you aren't reading carefully, he just quoted himself in this card. For Mother's Day, of course.

Enjoy the late great United States of America as it morphs into the Socialist USA. Words cannot help if all reasonable actions have failed. The Uzi and Magnum are the must have entities. Own one, learn to use it and carry it. You and your children will with reasonable probability need them sooner than later. Barry

Happy Mother's Day!

★ 6 ★

My Grandfather's Mouth

The most peculiar, sad, and entertaining part of living with a manic-depressive is the timing of erratic emotional behavior, whether it is up or down. My father has had some really impressively timed mood events.

The day I graduated from college my parents came to Boston for the commencement. It was a kind of miracle that I finished. I had the potential to be a perpetual student, the kind that would eventually have an office of some sort at the school. I did five years undergrad and there was really no way I could have strung it out any longer. I cobbled a major and minor together from the classes I took impulsively: English literature with a concentration on the Romantics, with a minor in film criticism. I don't even remember going to the yearlong Romantic poetry class because it was at 9 A.M. I have a vague recollection of cramming "Ode on a Grecian Urn" into my head and trying to read *The Cenci* in a night. I related to the poets, not necessarily their work, and that's what I wrote about in that class. I thought that was valid and I sold it. I graduated with honors, which was ridiculous. Charm goes a long way in the liberal arts.

My father was the valedictorian of his high school class. He came from a lower-middle-class upbringing and received a scholarship to college, then went on to medical school. His father was an odd-job bookkeeper and his mother was an elementary school teacher. I knew my grandparents a bit when I was younger. My grandmother seemed to be consumed with dread and worry and always in a panic about something. My grandfather didn't talk much and most of my memories of him involve him sitting quietly on the couch in his boxers with a bowl of summer fruit, eating nectarines with his large distended testicles hanging out of his shorts. My brother and I thought this was hilarious.

My father was the center of his family's attention, the wunderkind. His sister sort of faded behind his glory and became a teacher like her mother. He was mythic in the family. The doctor, the genius, the golden one.

I had lived with my father's erratic, selfish, sometimes abusive behavior all my life. It was always about him. A midlife diagnosis of bipolarity seemed to be his way of taking an easy out, at least in my mind. Initially I didn't buy the diagnosis. Even now, sometimes I don't know. It's very hard to determine the validity of a mood disorder when someone is as plain old narcissistic as my dad. I thought he was just a man-child who refused self-awareness and defied wisdom even as his life fell apart around him. When necessary he would blame the "illness."

When my folks showed up in Boston for my graduation, my father was close to despondent. It was supposed to be my day, but when we had a moment alone in the car, me sitting there in my graduation robe, my father looked at me and said, "I don't want to live anymore." Being used to this line of conversation, I said,

"You think you can make it one more day? I'm about to graduate."
I could usually make him laugh even at his lowest. That was sort
of my job.

What pissed me off about his timing, and I do believe it was
deliberate, was that if there was any day that really could revolve
around me it was this one. Instead, he disappeared that afternoon
into the city. My mother and I wondered if we should call the
police or check the bridges. While we paced around the street
panicking, he wandered back, just in time to suck the energy out
of the entire commencement ceremony. I believe everyone felt it.
Boston University president John Silber, who gave the address,
didn't have half the impact he would have had my father not been
sitting in the stadium. We're probably better off. Silber and a stadium could have led to something collective and dubious. It's
possible my father's involuntary needy Jewish dark magic saved
lives that day.

He also hijacked my first wedding. By then my parents were divorced and my father, though he was there with his new wife,
kept pestering my mother. He wandered around with a loose-leaf
binder of poems he had written, asking people if they wanted to
read them. The poems were horrible.

My father needs to have an effect on people. He needs to either
drag them down to his level or blast through them with his anger.
If he is in depressive mode, he is a gravitational force that pulls all
attention downward, toward him and his suffering. In manic
mode he needs other people to stop whatever they're doing and
regard him as a sage or wizard. I don't think this is unusual with
doctors, especially surgeons. When he is level he is just self-
involved and detached. The bottom line with my old man is that
he is an emotional terrorist. I love the guy, but it took a long time
to seal up the damage from the paternal storm that I went through

to get to my island. After a certain point I tried to focus on the positive elements of sharing genes with him. He's in his seventies and still has a lot of energy. He's very curious about things and speaks his mind. He doesn't have anything like the wisdom of age or hindsight. He's a biased historian of self, an emotional revisionist. We all are, for the most part.

)·

What you don't know about your parents is what becomes fascinating as you get older. They had a life before you were born and while you were growing up in the room down the hall and that was their business. My parents were very young when I came along, so the life before was limited to high school and college and whatever the hell went wrong in their childhoods. As to what happened to them after I was born, I've only gleaned bits and pieces, slipped moments.

I tend toward darkness in my amateur psychoanalytic practice. Since my parents are so crippled emotionally, I want there to be sordid sources for their behavior so I can respect them more and empathize instead of feeling mad and jilted. Obviously I will never know the most of it. I'm not sure they even do anymore. Things get lost as time dims the lights.

I'm curious and even inquisitive, but there's some stuff I really don't want to know about them. Parents seem to believe that there's an emotional statute of limitations on their secrets, but I think that's wrong: There's some stuff they should never tell you. But after a divorce, or years of bad blood, or a supersaturation of shame, or just old age, parents think the statute is up and they will dump some toxic garbage on your psyche's front lawn. For instance, I now know my father was a philandering madman. I've got details I can't even disclose here that involve guns and pissed-off husbands.

Then there was this conversation on the phone with my mother.

Mom: I just wanted to tell you I am going into the hospital overnight. Everything is fine. I just wanted you to know.

Me: What do you mean? What's wrong?

Mom: Nothing. Don't worry.

Me: Just tell me what's up. I can handle it.

Mom: I'm getting my boobs redone.

Me: Redone? What? When did you have them done originally?

Mom: Nineteen seventy-six. Right before your bar mitzvah.

Me: Really, you had like the original fake boobs.

Mom: Yes, the doctor said they needed to come out. They're calcifying.

Me: Okay, that's enough info. Well, let me know everything is okay.

I felt like my entire life was a lie. All those years I just thought my mom had great tits.

There are things I don't want to know about my parents, but I like knowing things about myself. This sometimes means tracking my behavior back to root causes, to my emotional legacy, which runs through my parents. Because of my mother's eating disorder I asked her if she had ever been sexually abused. She has become much more self-aware and quite pleasant and proactive about it. When I asked her, she said, "Ya know, Marc, I keep trying to remember something like that but I don't think so."

She blames her mean fat grandmother for it because she made my mother eat. I can handle that.

My father is a mystery to me, outside of knowing that he was the center of his family's attention and that he had a depressed mother, and perhaps a biological propensity toward depression. I never really had a sense of what his relationship with his father was. By the time I met my grandfather, Ben, he was a very passive man. My grandmother and the woman he married after my grandmother died were both incredibly overbearing in one form or another, from what I could tell. As I got older my father told me that he lost his virginity when his father got him a prostitute. I also picked up here and there that my grandfather was a bit of a lady's man and that caused some problems. That is really all I know. No real stories behind them, just information that I could enter into my emotional abacus. I'm always moving the beads around trying to figure out who I am.

With that said, I have never been able to explain to myself or anyone else what happened at my grandfather's funeral. It is an event that has become the epitome of the dark poetry that defines my relationship with my dad and his with his father. He dismisses it. I can't forget it. It defies meaning but craves it.

My grandpa Ben died from a stroke in 1992. I was on the east coast so I met my father at the funeral in New Jersey. I got to the funeral home to find that my father was manic, a normally strange disposition for a funeral, especially your own father's, but par for the course for my dad. He was making the rounds, telling jokes, laughing, checking in with people's lives. There was not a shred of grief in his behavior. To him it seemed like a fine time to be the center of attention. He was competing with the corpse and memory of his father. People act weird at funerals sometimes. Maybe he was consumed with sadness and this was a reaction to that. I don't think so. After he had been strutting around spinning yarns for a while I saw my father approach the funeral director, who was a tall, young woman with glasses. I walked over to make sure everything was okay.

We were standing in front of the closed doors of the chapel where the service was going to take place. My father said, "Can I see the body? I'd like to check something."

"Of course," the woman said with the morbid politeness of a woman who chose a morbidly polite occupation.

Jews don't do viewing. We do a plain pine box, closed. You remember your lost loved ones for who they were when they were alive. That's my understanding of it. But it is obviously a family member's choice to see a body.

"I'll go with you," I said. Not really to support my father but to buffer whatever might happen. He was very socially unpredictable in his manic states.

I had seen a body before. My high school buddy Dave died in the middle of the night of an asthma attack. I and a few other friends flew in from Los Angeles for the funeral. We got high before we went. It was an open-casket situation, although it didn't start out that way. In the middle of the service some guy just walked up to the coffin and flipped the lid. I walked quickly up to the casket and looked at my dead friend. The Jewish policy made sense to me in that moment. Everything I knew of Dave was erased in a flash and would forevermore fight with the image of the propped-up, overly made-up head now seared into my memory. Yeah, I got closure, but I had never doubted he was dead in the first place.

My father, the funeral director, and I walked into the empty chapel. The plain pine coffin was at the end of the room in front of the pews. We all stopped at the coffin. The woman stood to the side and lifted open the top half. My grandfather's face and upper body were wrapped in his tallis. She pulled back the shawl from both sides of his head, revealing my grandpa Ben's dead face. Eyes and mouth closed, lifeless. My father said, "It doesn't look like him."

I looked at my father and the funeral director, who said nothing. I let my father have his moment. My father then reached out his hand with a pointed finger and inserted his finger into his dead father's mouth and pulled it open.

"Dad, what are you doing? Dad?"

"Is there a problem with the mouth, sir?" the woman asked.

"No, it doesn't look like him."

My father was a doctor, of course, and there was something clinical about his prodding but that didn't explain anything. It was intrusive, disrespectful, and completely without boundary. I saw it as bizarre, a violation. Perhaps a small act of revenge for something I did not know or understand.

My father pushed the mouth shut. "It's him."

I was completely awed, stunned, and strangely energized by what Dad did.

"You can close it up," he said.

I thanked the woman, and my father and I started to walk out of the chapel.

"You all right?" I asked.

"Yeah, I just wanted to see his teeth."

We walked back into the main room, my father bounding ahead of me, ready to entertain the waiting crowd again.

★ 7 ★

Cats

I have become known for my cats because I have made my cats known. I talked about them constantly on my radio show and now on my podcast. I want it to be known now that I am not a "Cat Guy." I am a "My Cat Guy." I don't care about your cats. I will pretend to if I come over. I will say things like, "Awww, lookitthatguylookitthatnicecat." Secretly I will be thinking, "What a sad, fat, ugly dumb cat you have. Look at that thing. It's a feline train wreck. It looks like it's days away from hanging itself from its scratching post. It can't even muster up the gumption to play with what's left of that fake mouse you gave it. It doesn't go outside? It's just a hostage to your pain and neediness. Wow, you should probably put that cat down before it dies of ennui."

I don't say all that. I say, "Aw, lookitthatlittleguysocute."

I grew up with dogs, lots of dogs. Over the course of my childhood we had four Old English sheepdogs. A good part of my young life was spent covered in dog hair, cleaning up shit and pulling different-sized dogs off my leg. My father wanted to show dogs professionally. He was obsessed with it. As with all his obsessions—skiing, stereo equipment, cars, guns, vitamins—the family was just expected to fall in line behind his dog-show dreams.

I don't know why he chose Old English sheepdogs but he did. Our first was Mac Duff. Mac is the dog that set my father off on the addictive cycle of amassing dogs. It wasn't Mac's fault; Mac was a fun dog but he got cancer and my mother had him put down. He wouldn't be the last. Over time my mother became the Dr. Kevorkian of animals.

Mac Duff wasn't Mac's whole name. Breeders have this thing where a dog's entire genetic chain has to be represented in the name, for instance, our eventual champion Cheerio Lord Raglan. A royal name for a dog that was too genetically thoroughbred to be a good pet. Cheerio Lord Raglan was inbred and nervous, crazy even, but really beautiful. He didn't know his own strength and would snap at you for no reason. A bite from a stunning dog doesn't hurt any less. It's actually worse because you have to defer your pain to the privilege of owning a champion. You just have to suck it up. This dynamic also applies to living with beautiful women.

Our family vacations were centered around dog shows. It was all about the dog. There were travel cages, grooming tables, special leashes and food, and walks. There was a lot of brushing going on. My father would sit and brush a dog for what seemed like hours on the floor next to a pile of gray dog hair. It seemed like one of us should have been spinning it into yarn. All these vacations culminated with my father trotting around a ring like an idiot with a leashed and terrified mass of bouncing fur.

Then there was Samantha, whom my dad got suckered into buying from some cons who convinced him she was a show dog.

We thought Sam was a clean genetic machine. Turns out, not so much—her snout was too long, or maybe it was her brow. The point was, she had a flaw and that made her a pet disappointment. She seemed to know it, too, moping around in a lifelong apology for something that was out of her control, as so many of us do. Great dog, though.

Then we bred the Lord with some other guy's dog, which the owner claimed was of noble lineage, and got Disco, again not quite on the genetic money. Disco was nuts like her father but unshowable. By the time my father lost interest in showing and breeding dogs we had three: a retired champion, his townie wife, and a fucked-up kid from another marriage.

So I was never going to be a dog person; even my masochism and desire to revisit childhood trauma has its limits. But there were cats around in my childhood, too. My mother liked to talk to them. When asked why, she used to say, "They don't talk back." It usually took her three names to get to mine when she was calling out to me in the house, and two of them were animals. Still, I always liked the cats. There was Garfield, the large, lean field cat, and Gimper, the long-haired black princess with a limp. They weren't show animals; they were hunters and gatherers. We lived on three and a half acres so you never knew what they would bring home: lizards, snakes, birds, large bugs. It was always a treat to be presented with any of this vast array of dying gifts.

I once had an unforgettable, primal bonding moment with Garfield, a bizarre episode shared by two males of different species. I was visiting home one day after I'd already moved away and started doing stand-up. I was in my mid-twenties and had gone to do a set at a club in Albuquerque, New Mexico. I hooked up with one of the waitresses there and had no choice but to take her home to my childhood room for the sex. We had to be quiet because what was left of my parents' marriage was sleeping upstairs. In the middle of the hungry, grasping intimacy of two strangers having a go at it I heard Garfield come into the room. I lifted my face up and saw that he was carrying the corpse of the biggest field mouse I had ever seen. The thing was almost as big as the cat. He took it under my desk. The woman did not notice any of this.

I was stifling my sex noises, she was stifling hers, and Garfield was savaging a rat-sized mouse a few feet away. I could hear his snorting and tearing. I came like a teenager in his bedroom, a compressed and quiet climax so as not to wake up my parents. The woman and I got dressed and I walked her out. As I was walking down the hallway back to my room I saw Garfield walking out. I went in and looked under the desk and there on the floor, neatly arranged, was the tail, the head, and what looked to be a fetus of a field mouse. I wasn't disgusted. I was impressed. I felt that we had connected on the great timeless arc of animal drives. I didn't read too much into it other than the hope that it was a good omen. I hadn't used protection.

I went years without any pets, but in the middle of my divorce from my first wife, Kim, my then-girlfriend Mishna brought me a tiny black-and-white female cat I named Butch. I called her Butch because she had swagger. I was seeing Mishna while my divorce was being processed but she wasn't living with me. It was just Butch and me. She was a very small kitten and I wanted her to have everything. I went to holistic pet food stores and got her raw food so she would have the right bugs in her guts to survive outside if necessary. I even made her fresh cat food for a while but that proved to be ridiculous and she really didn't like it much. I think I wanted to treat Butch the way I wish I could've treated myself. I wanted life to be perfect for her since mine seemed to have crumbled. I invested a lot of love and caring into that cat.

When my divorce was complete Mishna and I moved to Los

Angeles from New York City. She left her Forty-sixth Street walk-up and I sublet my apartment in Astoria. It was a big ordeal. We rented a U-Haul, put all of our stuff in it, and set out. I had to get there in three days to make a meeting for a show I was trying to sell. In light of all the chaos, including the truck breaking down, our primary concern was Butch. I drove the truck and Mishna drove my old Honda Accord with the cat. Butch rode in the back of the Accord with a plant she had taken a liking to. She always slept in the pot of this plant, which was adorable. Of course in the car she had no use for it but I still have that plant.

After we made it out to L.A. we adopted a shelter cat called Boomer to keep Butch company. The cats at the shelter were mostly older cats. They looked as though someone had forgotten them or had had enough of them. There was one cat that seemed to be out of his mind. Completely nervous and unfriendly but young. I wanted that cat. That was Boomer. Having dealt with other cats since then, I know now that Boomer was feral. I liked his energy. I like anything I have to fight to get to like me. During this time we also found out that Butch had a genetic heart defect. Her heart was too big. The vet told us that she wouldn't live long.

Mishna and I got married in our backyard in L.A. and tried to build a life there. The problem was I wasn't working very much, so I decided to take a gig as the morning host on Air America, a new liberal-oriented radio network. I took the job hoping to take down the Bush administration but definitely to make money. The show was based in New York, but Mishna didn't want to join me—she was an actress, comedian, and screenwriter. An aspiring actress, comedian, and screenwriter. She wanted to be in L.A.

I still had the lease on the old beat-up apartment in Astoria so I moved back in, furnished it with IKEA garbage, and started the hardest job of my life. I would go to sleep at 8:30 P.M. and wake up at 2:30 A.M. to get it together to get to the studio by 4:00 A.M. Then I would start crunching the news with my staff and partner to get on the air with something to say by 6:00 A.M. After a few weeks of that schedule I became completely detached from regular life or my version of the same. There was no going out, there was no staying up, there was no real socializing except on the air and with my staff. I did stand-up on weekends. I never really felt rested. I was walking around like I'd just been in a long pillow fight, dazed but not hurt. All my energy went into keeping alert enough to function.

So now I was doing morning radio in New York while my wife was learning how to stop loving me in Los Angeles. The hours and distance were straining my marriage. The only time we could talk was right before I left the house. It would be 3 A.M. my time and midnight in L.A. and I would spend most of the conversation berating her for her imagined betrayals and unwillingness to do the only thing I wanted her to do: to care for me. It was deeply awful and I could feel the marriage disintegrating. I was a jealous, angry person. I knew that what was going on in my mind was not real but I could not stop it from coming out of my mouth. I kept finding myself at that horrible moment when you are about to say something hurtful to someone you love and you know you shouldn't but can't seem to stop it. You just watch it leave your mouth, hang in the air, and mold itself into a rock that plows into your lover's face. The phone connection was like a transcontinental slingshot. That was my marriage.

Then I would take a car into work, stopping on the way to pick up a large silo of liquid crack at Dunkin' Donuts and two packages of M&Ms. I would then caffeinate and sweeten myself into a mania amplified by exhaustion, by the angry fear that I was destroying my marriage, and by a deep hatred of all things Republican during the bleakest years of the Bush administration.

A few months into the job I got a call at the office at 4 A.M. from Mishna. She told me Butch had died. I was furious. She had been telling me for days that Butch seemed sick. I guess her large heart got too heavy and Mishna never got around to taking her to the vet. In my mind she had killed my cat. It confirmed my worst suspicions about our marriage. She only cared about herself and wasn't responsible enough to take care of a hurt animal. Me, or the cat. My cat was dead and my wife was a coldhearted child. She buried Butch with the help of Ernie the fix-it guy, in the same backyard that we'd gotten married in. I still regret missing the funeral of my cat. I think our marriage was buried that day, too. I hated Mishna.

As the months went by, things just deteriorated. Mishna would come to New York for a few days or I would go home for a few days but the distance between us became hard to navigate. I was lost, angry, and tired. About this time I began noticing a pack of stray kittens in the back of my building. I would go out in the middle of the night to put my trash in the bins and these five kittens would be scrambling around eating the garbage in the dark. They were so clean, cute, and focused. Like most of life, the scene was simultaneously adorable and awful. I thought to myself, "Someone better deal with this or these cats are going to fuck each other and we'll have an army of incested kitties out here."

This went on for a couple of weeks and I began to fall in love with these cats. There was this orange tabby with a tuft of hair on its nose that was a little asymmetrical and made him look like a monkey. There was a calico, a black-and-white longhair, a mean-looking, skittish striped cat, and this gray and white dwarfy fist of feline beauty that I would eventually name LaFonda. LaFonda is crazy, like Vietnam crazy. It's my fault.

Their mother was also around. The slut. I really didn't know what to do with the cats. They wouldn't let me get near them, but something had to be done about them. I just kept hanging on to the hope that someone else would deal with it. The truth is I was completely taken with two of these cats. I just thought they were too good to become alley cats. They were so perfect and clean and innocent that I didn't want them to live that harsh alley-cat life. I think the impulse to save animals is, aside from being empathetic and humane, also symbolic of saving some part of ourselves. I wanted these cats to be okay. I wanted to be okay.

The night before the 2004 Republican National Convention I was freaking out. We were going to cover the convention live at a booth in Madison Square Garden, behind enemy lines. I was nervous and couldn't sleep. So, of course, I decided I was going to deal with the cat issue. That's how I do. When life is scary and chaotic I like to make it more so.

I took a large shoe box and cut a hole in it. I put a small can of food in the box and set it out by the garbage can while I stood behind the basement door and watched. I had recruited my neighbor Jodi to help me; her job was to make sure I didn't completely freak out. I saw the first cat get in the box. I scrambled outside, quickly covered the hole in the box with a piece of cardboard, picked the box up, and ran it up two flights of stairs to my apartment. I released the animal into my place and it scurried scared and crazy behind the stove. "It's freaked out," I thought. It will grow to like me.

Over the next few hours I performed this same procedure with four of the five kittens. Once I finally had them in the house it was like I'd released a pack of wild ferrets into my living room. They weren't acting like house cats. I didn't realize at the time that if a cat is eating on its own it's not a cute housekitten: It's feral. I had trapped and released four wild animals into my apartment.

Two of them lodged themselves behind the stove. When I looked back there all I could see were two gaping, hissing mouths directed at me. The cat that I named Monkey went flying down the hallway and attempted to jump out a window. I was two stories up. He hit the screen, then climbed up the screen and wedged himself between the screen and the window. He stayed there for two days. LaFonda got herself stuck to a glue trap I had laid out for mice. She was flopping around on my kitchen floor, a mess of angry gray fur attached to a card. She didn't know me, I didn't know her, and I had to pull her off the trap. Her claws ripped through my hand but I managed to detach her from the goo plate. I believe the terror of that incident got locked deep in her wiring. She is still twitchy about it. That was her Nam.

In the days that followed I tried to shoo them back out the door but they didn't even know where they were so they wouldn't leave the apartment. I had no idea how to handle the situation. I tried to pull the "I'm your parent now" thing, but these cats were already about three months old; they weren't trying to hear that mess. I was surrounded by vicious little things and all I'd wanted was friends.

Night was the worst. The black-and-white cat whom I called Hissy would sit in the window of the kitchen, which faced out the back of the building. She would wail and her mother would answer in the alley. It was heartbreaking. I was living in a cat opera and I was the bad guy. The other one, whom I called Meanie, had a very frightening stink eye that he would shoot at me. He was horribly menacing for something that size. Monkey dislodged himself from the window, and LaFonda, after the mouse-trap incident, spent most of her time under the couch. When I shut the door to my bedroom to go to sleep, they'd all emerge. From under my covers, it sounded like my house was being ransacked and robbed. I would let it go on because I wanted them to have fun. When I woke up and walked into the living room there were no cats but half the couch was ripped open and the stuffing was all over the floor, books were destroyed, the rug was partially unwoven, and the TV was on.

I started talking about the cat crisis on my radio show. I was reaching out to cat ladies. Most big cities have a small army of middle-aged, usually single, misanthropic women who live for cats. I needed help. Emails started coming in. Someone donated two cages for my apartment to separate the cats and try to socialize them a bit. A woman came over with syringes and we put gloves on and inoculated the four kittens and took them to the vet to have them fixed. Another woman brought over traps and I trapped the mother and the other kitten and fixed them. I was doing good.

It was all I could talk about to anyone: on the radio, to my wife, to anyone who would listen. Cat tales. I think it actually may have bought more time in my marriage. I didn't have the mental space for jealousy. I was running a small veterinary hospital out of my apartment.

Needless to say, none of these cats was becoming any less wild and they all hated me. I was scarred and torn and discouraged. When I left Air America, I was confronted with the problem of what to do with the cats. I had done my best over the course of a few months, but now I was leaving New York and wasn't so sure that I wanted to bring a pack of wild animals with me. I loved a couple of them, though, and became intent on getting LaFonda and Monkey to Los Angeles. I found a woman who liked feral cats to take Hissy. Meanie was a disgruntled loner. There was no one who could tame that cat. So I tricked him into a box and took him to the Yemeni bodega across the street. They said they needed a mouser. I brought Meanie down into the basement of the store. The owner, Tony, put out a can of food and I said goodbye. I thought I would see him again. I went into that store all the time.

A few days later I went in to get some ice cream. I asked Tony how Meanie was doing. He said, "That cat is crazy. He's gone." I asked, "What do you mean?" He said, "He's in Brooklyn with my cousin."

I took that to mean the same thing as "he swims with the fishes." I don't think Tony killed the cat but I'm sure he sent it back out into the streets. It made me sad but I knew the cat was fixed and probably happier.

There was no way I was leaving Monkey and LaFonda behind. I loved just about everything about them and I needed them in my life despite the fact that they clearly had little to no interest in me. Much like the women I tend to fall in love with.

Raising feral cats was something I was getting used to, but transporting them was a whole other box of horror. Mishna flew out and picked up Monkey. She said it wasn't that big of a deal. But it was my job to carry the mighty LaFonda across country.

I was terrified of LaFonda. I still am. She is nothing but a ball of muscle and claws. The only time she had ever been in a cage was to go to the vet to get fixed, and it took two of us even to get her to do that and one of us was a registered Cat Lady. Now I was alone and completely panicked and tweaked. I put on leather gloves, got my mind into a "by any means necessary" state, and approached the cat. I wrestled her to the ground and picked her up with both hands. She bit through the gloves and lunged at my face, drawing blood on my arms with her claws and biting through thick leather into my hand. When I finally got her into the cage, she shit all over it. All my cats do that. As soon as I get them in the cage they evacuate their tiny cat bowels as if to say, "Fuck you! Who wins now?" Once I got her secured I bandaged my face, arms, and finger. There were scratches up and down both of my arms. But I'd completed my mission: I had courageously wrestled the wild into submission like some primitive. I felt connected to a tradition of men who hunted and led tribes. I had my bags packed and my cat boxed and I headed to JFK Airport for my flight.

Things were going pretty smoothly. I was waiting on the security line and was about to put the cat box on the belt to go through the machine when a Transportation Security Administration guy said, "You're going to have to take the cat out of the box and walk it through."

I said, "What? There's no way that is going to happen."

"Well, then you can't go through," he said.

"Do you know what I've been through? Look at my hands, look at my arms, look at my face! There's no way I'm taking that cat out of that box!"

I was yelling, waving my arms at the TSA dude.

People were looking at me, some shocked, others just perturbed. I was that guy. I was a crazy cat lady guy.

My biggest fear was that I would get her out of the case and she would jump out of my arms and my life would become a Disney comedy. I pictured a montage of me running after a cat on jetways, down the aisles of planes, in the middle of a runway, on aircraft wings, behind ticket counters, on a baggage claim.

I had made such a scene that when I went to take LaFonda out of the box the TSA guy said, "Okay, everyone stand back." Like I was defusing a bomb. I lifted little LaFonda out of the crate and she was more frightened than I was, but not much. I walked her quickly through the metal detector and then started screaming, "Where's the box!"

I didn't know at the time that all she would want to do was get back in the box. The airport was just a big blur of sights and sounds that were alien to her. The box, she understood.

I got her back in, sheepishly apologized to the agent and gawking passengers, and skulked away toward my gate.

We made it home and now my cats are free.

I lost a job, a marriage, and several pints of blood in the process, but they've won. They started in the garbage in Astoria, Queens, and now live in the hills of Highland Park, California. This is a cat success story.

★ 8 ★

Petty Lifting

I was back living in New York when I heard that Mishna, my second ex-wife, was living there with her new man. The divorce was still fresh and I had not been able to pull myself together for months. I knew that I would eventually run into her. I just didn't know when. How would it unfold? Would I be on the train? At a show? Carrying a cat in a cage? Holding a yoga mat? Would I yell, cry, avoid her? All of those? Would she be with her man? Would I hit him, yell at him, or cry at him? Maybe I would just yell at both of them. No. All the scenarios that I played out in my mind amplified the shame and sadness of my position. There was no winning because I had already lost, and at the center of any of the situations I imagined would be me, holding my own ass, which she had handed me.

I dreaded and hoped that I would run into my ex. Every day was an involuntary search to connect with her. It was the hidden agenda of my heart. I couldn't really focus on much else. I felt like I needed closure. I needed to be punched in the heart with the reality of the situation. That is what emotional connection is to me sometimes. Pain makes me know I am alive. Joy and comfort are awkward and make me want to die. I needed to see in her eyes that she didn't care about me and I had no power over her. Of course, I was hedging my bets. Some part of me hoped we would once again lock into that shared emotional frequency that undeniably connected us. I thought that connection was indelible, no matter what happened between us, even if it was like a tattoo that seemed like the right thing to do at the time but is now just a fading green mistake.

Worse than the feeling of loss that comes with a breakup is the feeling of losing. Loss is a state of emotional injury that you can get past; losing is a feeling of humiliation and defeat that stays fresh. The latter causes most of the problems in the world. If there is another man involved, it is almost impossible not to judge yourself as a failure and see him as an enemy.

Technology doesn't help. After my marriage ended, I set aside some time to work on a self-funded research project called "Who Is My Ex Fucking." It took about twenty minutes. I googled her name and searched images. I found a picture of her and a guy at an event. Their names were listed beneath the picture. I searched his name and within a few minutes I found out he was a Harvard graduate, a screenwriter, rich, and that his mother is a famous artist. The only consolation I had in that moment is that his credits were *eh* and he wasn't that attractive. It was a small consolation. Doing a Google search to find out things about your ex is similar to googling cancer when you think you have it. Depending on what you find, it can confirm in a moment that you are dying inside and there is nothing you can do about it.

I had flown my cat Monkey from California out to New York to stay with me. It is a sad situation when you are leaning on a cat for emotional support, but he showed up for me. Me and Monkey in Astoria, Queens, holding down the fort. It was a return to Monkey's roots. Out in back was the garbage can he had been eating out of when I found him. We were both at the source of a lot of past trauma and chaos. I don't think he hung on to his past as much I did. He had been eating out of the garbage. I was thrown away.

I had made a habit of compulsively checking the email that comes through my website. Trolling for validation, contempt, hate: the speedball of social networking in the age of accessibility.

A cryptic email showed up in the inbox. It was from a woman who said she would be in New York for a couple of days and wanted to have coffee with me. She was familiar with my radio work. She said she made a living off her image but she was getting a little "long in the tooth" for it. I had not heard that expression up until that point so I had to learn what that was. Initially I thought it was something frightening. The whole thing was a little mysterious: "images," long teeth, aging.

I googled her name and found a link to a modeling site. There was a portfolio of a model with her name and from the pictures, it appeared that she was a fairly successful one. I immediately thought that someone was pranking me, that it was a setup of some kind, but I was so sad and desperate for excitement and connection that the potential danger of the situation—both emotionally and physically—didn't stop me from setting up a meeting with this person.

I showed up at the coffee shop we had agreed to meet at in Soho. I looked around and saw a blond woman wearing old-lady glasses and sitting by herself. It was her. The woman from the modeling spread. It's always a little silly to see pretty women trying to unpretty themselves with glasses. Maybe that is just the way I see it. Maybe she was just wearing glasses because she has bad eyesight, and I was objectifying her. Of course that was it. But then objectification is a model's racket.

We talked for a few minutes. She said she was a fan of my radio work and used to come see me with her boyfriend when we did live shows and they lived in Brooklyn. I kind of remembered her. She had that strange mutant beauty that models have. It's the kind of beauty that no matter what they are wearing or how they try to hide themselves, a sharply defined, electric appeal comes through and zaps your desire.

She said she was still with her boyfriend but they lived out of state now. She was in town for a few days and wanted to hang out. I said, "Do you mean *hang out* hang out?" She said they had an open relationship and that as long as she was honest about what she was doing it was cool. I didn't ask for too much explanation. It felt a little weird. I wondered if he was aware of the status of their relationship but I didn't mention that. I was in.

I really couldn't believe it was happening. I felt I had won some kind of prize. I had been so beaten down by myself since the split that I had no sense of self-esteem left, and I really hadn't had much to begin with.

We left the coffee shop and went back to my apartment. We had insanely deep, amazing sex. We danced in my living room. I smoked a cigar naked in my kitchen and watched her do an improvised nude mambo to Tito Puente music coming out of the radio on top of the fridge. It was one of those moments I realized that I could be anywhere—a castle, a yacht, a private jet—but it wouldn't get any better than that moment. It would not be any better than what was going on in my dirty beat-up Astoria kitchen. That is the power beautiful women have: They are portals into the timeless, into other worlds. And I had needed very badly to get out of this one.

We spent a couple of days together. I knew that was all I had. I felt grateful and stupid. That is what beautiful women do to me even if I don't know them. Does that make me shallow or just a man? I don't know.

The last day she was in town she and I were walking arm in arm down Fourteenth Street. We were just talking and laughing, knowing this would be our last day together. About a half block ahead of us I sensed a familiar frequency moving toward us, a form, a person whom I had motion memory of. It was my ex. This was the moment. Could there have been a better one? No. I see her just as she sees me. The woman and I move past her. The woman does not know what is happening. I am watching my ex-wife as she watches me and we pass each other. Nothing is said. I look back and she gives me a "what the fuck" look. I turn away and start giggling. The woman I was with asks, "What are you laughing at?"

"An amazing thing just happened. That was my ex that just walked by. I haven't seen her in over a year. The fear has been lifted! Thank you."

She didn't quite know what I was talking about but I felt my heart open in relief. At least I could save a little face. Not that it mattered, really. In retrospect her look could have been shock that I didn't stop and introduce her and not what I assumed and wished she was thinking at that moment, which was:

"You have moved on and replaced me with someone just as beautiful."

It was all so shallow, so relieving, so petty, so perfect.

★ 9 ★

Guitar

I play guitar. I play a lot. I play when feelings build up in me and I need to put them out in the world in a safe way. Guitar is the only method of meditation that I have. I do it alone. I do it well enough for it to work. I wasn't always like that.

I was forced to play guitar. When I was kid there was an old Harmony hollow-body guitar with f-holes lying around the house that belonged to my father, who, I assume, at some point got manic and obsessed over guitar, took some lessons, then abandoned it. Judging by the songbooks that were lying around my father wanted to be Pete Seeger. I guess he saw himself as an everyman lunatic bard, singing about the struggle of the self-obsessed.

I was about ten years old when my brother and I started taking lessons. Like any other activity my mother encouraged, I don't think it was about anything other than it meant she didn't have to deal with us. This was the same incentive for her to send us to camps (two different ones in one summer), swim team, Hebrew school, and actual school.

I don't know where my mom found our guitar instructor but he was a large, bearded, fat Christian hippie with horn-rimmed glasses named Brad and he had a tiny, portly wife named Claudia. Over the few years that he taught us guitar they became caretakers for us. My mother would build a day around keeping us out of the house. Brad and Claudia would pick us up from school or swim practice, take us out to dinner or prepare it for us, take us to their house for a lesson, and then take us home. It was odd.

Brad collected records and Claudia was an artist. There was a lot of sitting on cushions and eating vegetarian food. Brad was not a great player but he was a patient teacher and he liked to get us singing. I learned the basics from him. Chords and songs. He also introduced me to music I had never heard, Sonny Terry and Brownie McGhee. Blues music struck something deep within me. I really don't know why but I felt the rawness and mystery of it. Voices crying out of a place so far beyond my understanding, certainly as a ten-year-old, moved me. I innately understood the flow of the music. I have a blues-based brain and I have to thank Brad for turning that on. The depth of my appreciation continues to expand as I get older. I don't listen to much new stuff, but the stuff I do listen to gets deeper every time I hear it, which I think is a testament to the genius of the form if you don't trivialize it. Bad bar bands killed the blues for many people for many years, which is a shame.

Once we were back at home, my mother would force us to practice for fifteen minutes every night. My brother and I would sing together and fight over which songs to play. Eventually we figured out how many times we could play "Take Me Home, Country Roads," "Rocky Raccoon" and "Johnny B. Goode" to eat the time.

In my freshman year of high school I auditioned for stage band but couldn't get in as a guitar player because all I knew how to play was chords, and not many of them. I told the conductor that I could play bass. He said if I promised to learn how to read music I could be in the band. I said sure. Needless to say I never learned how to read music, because getting high with friends and driving around doing nothing was more important. We got our licenses at fifteen in New Mexico. It was insane.

I became the bane of that conductor's life. He hated me. I would stand in the back of the band with my Hohner copycat bass that I bought off Brad and try to improvise, having no idea how to play bass, not a clue as to how to read music, and certainly no ability to improvise. There was another bass player who would stand there with me. He had no idea what he was doing either, but we were both getting some kind of credit. We would take turns fucking up the rhythm section. It was embarrassing.

We did a lot of traveling as a family. We had a Caprice station wagon and my brother and I would lie in the very back listening to the eight-tracks that my father rotated through. The ones that had the most impact on me were the soundtrack to *American Graffiti, Abbey Road, The Buddy Holly Collection, Simon and Garfunkel's Greatest Hits,* and "Hocus Pocus" by Focus. There were some duds, like *The Best of Bread* and Mac Davis's *Greatest Hits,* but "Guitar Man" was kind of touching and "Baby, Don't Get Hooked on Me" seemed curious and sordid to my ten-year-old mind and anything to accelerate puberty was welcomed at that time. *American Graffiti* was my dad's music. He loved it. I still know every song on that soundtrack. There were two Chuck Berry tunes, "Johnny B. Goode" and "Almost Grown." "The Stroll," "Get a Job," "Chantilly Lace," "Surfin' Safari," "Party Doll," "Peppermint Twist," "Maybe Baby." My dad would sing along with all of them. The songs meant something to him. I wanted them to mean something to me so I could mean something to him. Now they do.

I became morbidly obsessed with the Big Bopper, Buddy Holly, and Ritchie Valens after my father told me they had been killed in a plane crash and how upsetting it had been to him. When I heard their songs, they were saturated with death. When I looked at the picture of Buddy Holly on the cover of the eight-track it filled me with dread and horror. Buddy Holly was the sound of the dead to me. All his songs were haunted. It was the same with Janis Joplin. My parents had the vinyl of *Pearl,* with the beautiful picture of Janis on the chaise longue on the cover. My mother told me that she died of a heroin overdose. In my mind Janis was heroin. That's what it looked like. The Full Tilt Boogie Band were smack's supporting players. I was fascinated with dirty hippies and drugs. They seemed to have figured it out.

The Chuck Berry songs also got under my skin. I was already stuck on that two-string opening to "Roll Over Beethoven"—one of the first records I owned for myself was *The Beatles' Second Album,* and out of all the songs on that record their cover of "Roll Over Beethoven" just killed me. I sought other versions of it. I was nine and I had my grandmother buy me a Mountain album because they did a cover of it. I finally arrived at Chuck's with his live *London Sessions* version, and then later in the car with my dad's *American Graffitti* album, my fixation was set. To me that riff was the gateway to everything. I was obsessed with it. I had no idea how to play it. It seemed impossible. I couldn't get beyond chords under Brad's tutelage.

The guitar player in my high school stage band was a Latino kid named Adolfo. He had perfectly feathered hair that he was always combing with a large comb that stuck out of the back pocket of his bell bottoms. I stood behind him watching his hand move up and down the neck effortlessly. Once on a break I mustered up the courage to talk to him. It was hard, because the entire band sort of hated me because I sucked and I was holding them back. I really just wanted to be kicked out. It was very stressful.

"Adolfo, do you like Chuck Berry?" I asked, shyly.

He clearly didn't want to be seen talking to me, so he answered me but didn't actually look at me. It was like I wasn't there.

"My old man does."

"So does mine! Do you know how to play 'Roll Over Beethoven'?"

Then, like magic, without even thinking about it, he laid into that opening riff. I was stunned and awed. I asked him to show me how to do it. He did, but he still wouldn't look at me or let me touch his guitar. I went home and tried it, it worked, and the entire world changed. I had it, the key to music. I was ecstatic. I was probably the only fifteen-year-old kid in the world in 1977 who was beside himself because he could play a Chuck Berry lick.

My first electric guitar was a Les Paul Deluxe copycat. Then I moved from Chuck to Keith Richards and I bought my first Telecaster when I was sixteen—just like Keith's. My brother let the guitar go in favor of a tennis racket and I moved on to another teacher, Vaughn. I started going to this music store that was owned and run by an aggravated, bitter jazz drummer, a wiry little balding man with a large moustache who always seemed pissed off. He had studios in the back for teachers. Vaughn was a tall, lean dude with a frizzed and wavy bleached-blond perm. He had a moustache and glasses and smoked Marlboro Lights. He played in a band and he became my mentor.

Vaughn would let me smoke while he taught me how to play lead. The approach was, I would bring in a piece of music on tape, play it for Vaughn, and he would figure it out and try to teach me. What usually happened is I would watch Vaughn figure it out and be amazed that he could. I would try to play it once, badly. He would be encouraging. Then we would smoke and he would listen to my teenage problems and talk me through them for the rest of the lesson, that is, most of the lesson. I learned my pentatonic blues and country scales and moved on. My guitar playing skills leveled off.

I had the basics and I had heart. I was never disciplined enough or enough of a nerd to master the guitar, or anything really. I just needed to know enough to express myself, to get me out there, out of myself, to be heard and to feel something. I could never focus on learning leads or playing songs correctly. I was always an interpretive player. I would find a song I loved and play a version that was good enough for me. I was only in a band once, in ninth grade, and we only knew four songs. We went through several band names but the song count stayed the same.

We had one gig as a band that I can remember. We said we would play at one of those parties where a family had just moved out of a house and one of the kids got hold of the keys and had half his high school over to destroy the house. I'm not sure what the band was called at the time. I think we were Change. Our regular bass player, Lee, wasn't available to play that night. He was a sweet guy who wore a floppy hat. He always seemed to have a good time bouncing around smiling like a teenage hippie clown. I think we played four times with him total, so it wasn't like he was irreplaceable. The other bass player we knew was this guy Monte. He said he could fill in for the gig. We all got to the house and Monte had a lot of equipment. He had a bass, an amp, and a couple of other large console components that I didn't recognize. He looked like he hadn't slept in days. He had dark circles under his eyes. He was wearing a big down jacket and chain-smoking Marlboros. I had never met him before and I can't seem to forget him. He laughed out of context.

I remember we were in the basement playing our four songs:

"Takin' Care of Business," "The Needle and the Spoon," "Sweet Emotion" and "Tush." Monte was great, better than the rest of us. We put our instruments down and we all disappeared into the drunken throng to try to make out with girls, drink keg beer, and/or help destroy the house. About five minutes had passed when an explosive sound came from the stage. It was jarring. Everything stopped, as if something horrible was about to happen. Then there was a thunderous cacophony of rapid-fire bass notes that began to loop and echo. The house was literally shaking. The source of the sound stood solitary in the corner of the basement where we had been playing. It was Monte. The assault of bass went on for about fifteen minutes, building layers of looping bass noise that peaked like an earthquake. Nobody knew how to process it. I had never seen anything like it. When he stopped no one clapped. No one talked. He put his bass down and walked through the crowd and out of the house. I followed him. We stood outside. He lit a cigarette and started laughing and said, "I'm on acid." It was one of those moments when I knew there was something out there that was wild, unmanageable, and accessible to me; if I hadn't been paralyzed with fear of it I would have been there in a flash.

I used to buy *Guitar Player* and eventually became something of a gearhead, one of those guys who hangs around guitar stores. I was fascinated and obsessed with equipment. I had gear that I didn't know how to use, really: wah-wah pedals, distortion boxes. I'd save up a ton of money and get something custom-made. I took the neck from my Telecaster and I put it on a Schecter Explorer body and had the guys at the shop refinish it. I finished it off with some fancy pickups, but I could never play that thing beyond my basic knowledge. I could never live up to my guitar. When I was sixteen I wished I was a wizard, but I never had the focus.

I eventually put the Tele back together, had it painted candy-apple red, put a brass pick guard on it and two humbuckers, and just loved looking at it. I still had that guitar in college, when I sold it for drug money to a guy who used to sleep on my couch. It was his first guitar and he loved it so I didn't feel so bad. He was a genius, just not a guitar genius. He's a pretty important poet and cultural critic now. I went to a reading he did at the New School in New York, and I was like, "What happened to that guitar?" And he said that his buddy's daughter's in a lesbian punk band, so he gave it to her. I felt pretty good about where it ended up.

More than a musician, I've been an obsessive fan. Throughout high school I was obsessed with the Rolling Stones, the Beatles, Tom Waits, Bowie, Eno, Muddy Waters, Iggy, Skynyrd, and on and on. Sometimes I would just become obsessed with an individual song. I would play the records over and over again, the music like an aural IV that changed my brain chemistry and paced my heart, taking me where I needed to go depending on my mood. There was driving music and there was sad music. Driving had to be done and sadness needed to be managed. Music transformed both into magical journeys. Add drugs to either and you had a day's activities on your hands, if not a lifetime's.

By the time I got to college I had a fairly arrogant attitude about music and my place as a music critic. Before I left home I had become friends with an avant-garde musician in Albuquerque who led me through the noise: Fred Frith, the Residents, Robert Fripp, the Eno ambient albums, Jon Hassell. In college, in Boston, I became coke buddies with a guy named Bill who was tied into the art scene and loft music movement there in the mid-eighties.

One night I was at a party with Bill at a loft. I was maybe twenty, he was a bit older. I thought I could hold my own with artsy types. I had known them in Albuquerque when I was growing up. Hell, I thought I was one. The pretension was thick, as it always is with unknown and struggling artists. Most of their energy is dedicated to crafting an aesthetic disposition in preparation for the day when people actually begin to buy their bullshit, if they ever do. I was sitting next to a heavy guy wearing horn-rimmed glasses. This was like 1983, so it was long before the horn-rim explosion that we are just now seeing ebb. He was talking about local bands and declaring certain bands transcendent, misunderstood.

I blurted out, "There's never going to be another Buddy Holly. He was the best."

Horn-rimmed face snapped back, "You're a fascist."

Bill stepped in and changed the subject, but I was hurt and shocked. I had no clear idea what fascism was at the time, but I knew I'd been slagged in front of Bill and his ridiculous friends. We left the party, but I couldn't get what that guy said out of my mind for twenty-five years. It was genius. He had shaken my worldview with those three words. It had been drilled into me by the ghoulish mythmaking of the music industry and by my own father that Holly was the best, a martyred god. Horn-rims committed an act of deicide and patricide all at once. But he did create room in my mind for new things. That's where Lou Reed came in.

I had been into Reed's Bowie-produced *Transformer* album, but when my buddy Rob gave me *1969: The Velvet Underground Live* my mind was blown. So simple, so layered, so nasty. I had to have everything they did. They represented a gritty New York psychosexual dark good time that I missed and yearned for though I probably couldn't have cut it had I lived through it. That's what your heroes do for you—lift you victoriously above the dirty work of life and conjure a different way of being.

This was what music was to me, magic. But it was a kind of magic I wanted to actually touch myself. It's the irony or maybe the tragedy of being a fan that it's not enough to let the music enter you like a drug or define and shape the world for you. You also want to somehow touch it and have it affirm you in more direct ways, whether you're playing a riff like Chuck Berry or singing like Buddy Holly or buying Keith Richards's guitar—or actually meeting your idols.

In 1984 Lou Reed came to Boston to sign his album *New Sensations* at Strawberry Records in Kenmore Square, which at the time still had some grit to it. I had to go. I thought, "I'm going to go meet Lou Reed. What do I wear? How do I make an impression? How do I get Lou to validate me?" Some part of me believed it was just going to be him and me and we were going to have a conversation.

I got to Kenmore Square and saw a line of people stretching out the door of Strawberry Records and winding down the street. I got on line behind a six-foot-five guy wearing a white jumpsuit. He had an amp strapped to his back and was playing Velvet Underground songs on his guitar. He was freakish looking. I should have spaced myself a few people behind him but I was excited. I didn't know how I was going to follow that. I assumed that Lou would just move him along. A one-man tribute wearing a mock space suit is not necessarily the most flattering honor. I figured those kinds of people had to frighten Lou Reed because their weirdness wasn't sexy, just weird.

I wasn't too worried. All I was thinking about was what I was going to say to Lou. How was I going to connect? I'd only have a moment to do it. My mind kept cycling through possibilities as I waited on line for about forty-five minutes, grasping my *Transformer* album in my sweaty fan hands. I finally got to the counter. I picked up *New Sensations* out of the bin on the way up. Some members of his new band grabbed both it and *Transformer* from me and signed both. Wait, what did they have to do with *Transformer*? It pissed me off.

I finally got down the line to Lou. We were face-to-face. I hand him my records and I say, "How are you doing, Lou?"

He says, "Good, man. What's your name?"

I say, "Marc."

He says, "Hey, Marc, how are you doing?" as he signs my records.

I say, "Pretty good, Lou." There's a beat. I seize my moment.

"Hey, Lou, what gauge pick do you use?"

A little guitar talk. That was my big question. That was what was going to set me apart from the rest of the fans. And God bless Lou Reed, because he looked at me and said, "Medium, man, you've got to use a medium."

Contact. I've been using a medium pick ever since.

10

Lorne Michaels and Gorillas, 1994

My mother always told me that I was a diaphragm baby. Which in my mind means I have an innate ability to overcome obstacles. In a race of 400 million, I was the winner. And *then* I had to bust through a diaphragm. God, I was ambitious when I had a tail. I had a biological imperative then, a goal. It was my job to propel bipolarity and a slight underbite into the next generation.

As an adult I have been passionately banging and thrashing up against the ovum of show business for twenty-five years. I've been passionately banging and thrashing in general. It's what I do. It is not unusual. I know you've probably heard that in show business it can take twenty years to create an overnight success but what you don't hear is that that is the exact same amount of time it takes to create a bitter failure. You just don't know what it's going to be until the night before. It doesn't have to be brought on by anything specific. Dreams don't die with any sort of cacophony; there is no parade. The wind is just sucked out of you in a last sigh and you surrender.

I'm beginning to realize that some things aren't going to happen the way I had planned. That's part of being an adult. All right, maybe I'm not going to be an astronaut. I'm going have to let that go. I'll put it on the back burner. I'll be mature about it, keep it as a hobby.

Some people don't even realize they're bitter. If you don't know whether you are or not, here's a quick quiz you can give yourself. If you ever wake up in the morning and the first thing you say is "Oh, fuck, not again," you might be a little bitter. If you find yourself in conversation with someone you know and that person brings up someone you both know and before he says another word you mutter, "That guy's a fucking asshole," you might be a little bitter. If you find yourself dismissing universally acclaimed landmark achievements, saying, for example, "*The Godfather* is an okay movie," you might be bitter.

Everyone is a little bitter. We're born bitter. The personality itself is really just a very complex defense mechanism. A reaction to the first time someone said, "No, you can't." That's the big challenge of life—to chisel disappointment into wisdom so people respect you and you don't annoy your friends with your whining. You don't want to be the bitter guy in the group. It's the difference between "I've been through that and this is what I've learned" and "I'm fucked. Everything sucks." That said, be careful not to medicate bitterness because you've mistaken it for depression, because the truth is, you're right: Everything does suck most of the time and there's a fine line between bitterness and astute cultural observation.

I had many dreams as a teenager. One was to be an artist—any kind of artist, preferably a comic. And if I was a comic, I wanted to be on *Saturday Night Live*. I loved John Belushi and Chevy Chase. Nowadays, that dream doesn't even make sense to me: I never really did characters other than the one I am becoming and I certainly haven't watched the show in years. But back in 1994 it almost happened. I had a meeting with Lorne Michaels.

Lorne had seen me a couple of times and was considering me for the cast of *Saturday Night Live*. Along with *SNL*, Michaels produced *Late Night with Conan O'Brien*. I had appeared on the O'Brien show the night before the meeting. I was feeling like a player. I had smoked a little weed that morning so I was a little buzzed. I was also reading Bruce Wagner's *Force Majeure* and there were times when I wasn't real clear whether I was a character in the book or what was happening was really happening. I was on the precipice of realizing a dream I had since I was a teenager. I had been waiting in the *SNL* lobby for about an hour and a half when the head writer of the show came out. He seemed more nervous than I was and stammered out, "Okay, he's ready to see you."

It was a private meeting in Lorne's office. I walked in with the writer and Lorne was putting something on a bookshelf. Lorne Michaels is a big presence. He's not really fat or tall, but in showbiz he is a god, possibly self-appointed. The head writer and I are standing there and he doesn't acknowledge us. He just continues to work at the bookshelf. He has heard us walk in. It is already awkward.

The head writer is seeming increasingly nervous and eventually says, "Lorne, Marc Maron is here."

Lorne turns around and says, "How was *Conan* last night?"

"Fine, it was good. It was."

"Did they *laugh* at you? Were they *laughing*?"

I looked at the head writer like *what the fuck?*

"Yeah, I did pretty well."

"It's better when they *laugh*, isn't it?" he says.

"Yes, it is," I said.

Then Lorne turns around and says, "I don't know what you

think you are doing down there below Fourteenth Street, but it doesn't matter."

A few days before the meeting I had been featured with some other comics in a *New York Times* piece about the burgeoning alternative comedy scene on the Lower East Side. In retrospect, telling me this might have been the only reason Lorne had me into his office. He wanted to school me.

The meeting was off to an awkward start.

That was the beginning, weird. Then we all sit down. I'm there in front of his desk. In front of me, right behind a picture that's facing him, there's a little bowl of candy. I was tweaking about the whole situation. So everything suddenly felt very loaded and I was thinking, *I'm not going to take any fucking candy. It's a test of some kind. He's testing my self-control. But how could that be the case given this show's history? Maybe I should take the entire bowl and put it in my mouth and dance around the room like a clown. Then I'll definitely get the show. I can't talk with candy in my mouth.*

I became very self-conscious.

I leave my head and check back into the situation at hand and Lorne is philosophizing. He speaks like everything he says is to be taken in on a very deep level. He is a man who clearly has the last word. He was in the middle of a long discourse that I had missed because I was thinking about the candy. He is saying, "You know, comedians are like monkeys."

I laugh uncomfortably.

"People go to the zoo and they like the lion because it's scary. And the bear because it's intense. But the monkey makes people laugh."

I just couldn't stop myself and I said, "Yeah, I guess if they're not throwing their shit at you."

It was an awkward moment, more awkward than the rest of the moments leading up to that one. Lorne seemed taken aback for about a second and then commenced to stare directly into my eyes for a long time. So long that the head writer fidgeted in his chair and laughed uncomfortably and said, "Lorne?"

Lorne said, "You can tell a lot from someone's eyes."

I was in a staring contest with one of the most powerful men in show business. I tried to exude some starness from my face.

Uncomfortable, I blinked and I took a candy.

As soon as I took the candy I swear to God Lorne shot a look at the head writer that clearly meant that I had failed the test. I walked out of there thinking I had ruined my career because of a Jolly Rancher. I don't even like Jolly Ranchers. I festered about it for days.

The day after I had the meeting with Lorne Michaels, the day after I felt myself on the precipice of something great, I had to go to Washington, D.C., to perform. I was the big headliner at the Comedy Cafe. What I didn't know until I got there was that it was the last weekend the club would be open and they didn't want to blow any money on publicity.

The first night, Friday night, first show, nine people. Not the worst thing in the world but as a comic, rarely do you walk off-stage after performing for nine people saying, "Fuck yeah! God, I made the right career choice! Man, I feel good about myself."

Second show, three people; three. One of them was the opener and he heckled. So needless to say, after meeting with Lorne and having this experience at the club I wasn't feeling great about myself.

After the shows I was feeling low so I went down to the strip bar next door, which was owned by the guy who owned the comedy club. It was one of these really sad, old strip bars where they have one stage and three girls. Men had to stand in line like some sort of religious procession to tip the woman, to honor the goddess of the pole.

So it's bad enough that we were sitting in the dark corners of the strip bar, but then we all had to get in line in the light and meekly make an offering. I didn't want to be there. It wasn't working. I was looking for some warmth, some affection, some love. If part of the stripper's job was to come up and say, "You're really funny," I would have been fine with that. That would have helped. But strippers don't say that unless you date them and that comes with a whole other bag of problems.

I was sitting in the back of the strip club looking vulnerable with the book I was reading at the time, *The Poetry of Arthur Rimbaud,* when one of the girls asked me if I wanted a table dance.

I agreed. She started dancing for me. I tried to focus. I made small talk. I said, "What do you do during the day?"

She put her tits in my face and said, "I'm a student."

"What do you study?" I said, face full of boobs.

"English literature," she said as she stood up, turned around, and bent over and shook her ass at me and spanked it. She looked back over her shoulder and said, "I'm minoring in political science."

"Nice," I said.

She turned back around and stood in front of me. She cupped one of her breasts with her hand, pushed it up, bent her head down toward the breast, and said, "On weekends I work with autistic children."

Then she licked her nipple.

I gave her twenty bucks, for the kids.

I left the strip bar feeling worse than before, because I wanted to fuck. I went to a convenience store and I loaded up on the low budget antidepressants: cigarettes, chocolate doughnuts, dirty magazines, soda. I just got this bag of junk and went to my hotel room and started in.

I was reading a magazine, I was listening to a CD on my Discman, I was smoking a cigarette, drinking coffee, having a doughnut, and watching television all at the same time. I was like some sort of many-armed Indian god, the Vishnu of self-avoidance. If

Sinbad's ship were sailing past my cave and his crew looked in, one of them would say, "It is the beast with many arms. We should kill it."

Sinbad would reply, "No need. He is dangerous only to himself."

It wasn't enough. I didn't have any drugs or alcohol, or else it would have been a very different party. It was my first attempt at sobriety. It didn't stick that time but I eventually got it.

It was just a sad, desperate situation.

Then something amazing happens. This show comes on television and it's about gorillas. It's about people helping gorillas in the jungle. Helping gorillas find better living environments. Helping the gorillas to have better lives in their gorilla worlds. As I watched I felt moved. It was one of those moments that seemed beyond coincidence, like my purpose was unfolding before my eyes. Those moments usually happen when I am annihilated with enough despair to think, "Oh, my God! That's what I should be doing. I should be out in the jungle with a shirt with a lot of pockets and a pith helmet helping monkeys."

I had to stop myself before I started making the phone calls because I didn't want to scare my friends. "Guess what? I'm quitting comedy. No, gorillas. I'm helping the gorillas now. No, I'm fine."

I've had moments like that before.

Then the screen fades to black and the title IVAN'S STORY comes up in white letters. It was about this sad gorilla in this concrete environment. He had no toys and he'd been there for twenty years. Just an old, neglected gorilla at a roadside attraction zoo, not even a real zoo. One of those places you see billboards for along the highway in the middle of nowhere: GAS, FOOD, SEE A LIVE GORILLA. And he was just sitting there in what appeared to be a cell, tapping on the wall. I thought maybe at a different time it was a much more passionate display of anger but years and repetition had rendered it an empty existential hobby.

I realized why this suddenly seemed so important. *I* was Ivan. I was disappointed, despairing, and tired of fighting. I was in a cage of my own making, unable to get out. People would pay to see me and leave sad and disappointed. Then I realized Ivan didn't have porn.

I switched the channel to the filthy menu. Now everything was going. It was just awful. Hotel room porn is the worst. I'm not delusional. I know I'm not watching healthy people. But porn is comforting. Yet another empty victory in the war against self. When it's over, the instigators of the battle are still fucking on the TV, mocking me.

Then I stopped and considered myself sitting there on my bed, surrounded by my elaborate array of empty existential hobbies. And I thought again about that abandoned monkey, and actually had a bonding moment with him. We're really not that different from monkeys. What's the difference? Pants? What's the difference between grunting and "Oh, email." If Ivan had a monitor in his little cell he'd see me just sitting there flaunting the full range of distractions that pants-wearing civilization offers us. A Discman, a laptop, a remote. My cell.

It was awful. I turned it off and I went to sleep. The next morning I had to get up and do morning radio at six o'clock. I get there and I'm all covered with a fine film of sugar, cum, hotel room air; it's just disgusting. My hair is fucked-up and it's all just hammering into me the truth: that I once thought I was going to do something great in this life and it isn't working out.

Chuckling Dumbfucks in the morning on Hot one hundred point who gives a shit. With morning radio there's always a guy with a regular name and then the Something Man. So I'm sitting there with Bob and the GasMan thinking, If Rimbaud were alive he wouldn't have had to do this . . .

"So Artie, you're in town doing some poetry, huh?"

An array of sound effects ranging from farts to yawns steps on Rimbaud's poem about farts and yawns.

After the radio show I walked around the capital, cold and dirty, picturing monkeys on the National Mall. The Founding Fathers.

I went into the National Gallery to see the Vermeer exhibition. His paintings elevate the mundane into timeless visual poetry. Art like this is the real separation between monkeys and man. The paintings seemed to be mocking me with their beauty and depth. I walked by the canvases looking at title cards. They blurred when I tried to read them: *What Did You Do Today? Look at You, Sad Man. Did You Masturbate in a Hotel Room Last Night?* I rubbed my eyes and then they came clear. *Girl Asleep at Table, Woman Pouring Milk, Woman Combing Her Hair, Woman Holding Balance, Woman in Blue Reading a Letter, Head of a Young Girl.* Simple moments stolen, rendered, eternalized.

I walked into the rotunda of the National Gallery and there was a girls' choir singing Christmas carols. What seemed like a hundred teenage girls stood in tiers belting out the festive songs. I stood there like some exhausted, debauched troll trying to fight the fantasy of them all standing there naked. I knew people could see in my face the unbridled frustration of the sad, tired, compulsive man in his overcoat.

I distracted myself with the sculptures. One was clearly a young girl barely clothed. It was beautiful and there was no shame in looking at that. I wondered if that was what was driving the artist. Was he just chipping away angrily with pent-up desire on his face thinking, "God, I want to fuck her"? That is where most creativity comes from.

That night I get to the club, and the restaurant connected to the showroom is packed. I get excited. Then I notice there's a guy in a gorilla suit dancing around presenting someone with some balloons and throwing candy around. It was a private party. I have a moment. I look at the guy in the gorilla suit and think, "That's that guy's job." That moment is followed immediately by the thought, "My job is really not that far from that." I'm just one or two evolutionary steps away from dancing around in a monkey suit with balloons. There is a fine line between telling jokes and smelling your own breath inside a plastic head. At least with stand-up comedy you have some choices. I can be on TV, I can write my own material, I can comment on the world, and I can express myself. Where's the room for creative growth in a gorilla suit? When was the last time someone said, "The guy in the monkey suit is a genius." Certainly not since Roddy McDowall.

I pictured the sad moment when the guy is at home after the gig. The head is on the coffee table and he thinks, "Hey, this is working out. This is the last time I rent. I'm going get my own suit."

I made my way through the crowd. I passed the man in the gorilla suit and walked into the showroom. That night I did one of the best shows I'd ever done, for twenty-three people. It came from someplace real.

The other thing I learned about show business recently is the difference between art and entertainment. Sometimes they meet but not usually.

I had an experience that fully illustrates this dichotomy. I was in Montreal at the annual comedy festival, and they have a lot of street performers in Montreal, a lot of buskers I guess is the proper word, a romantic term for mimes and whatnot.

I was walking down the street and there was this huge crowd in the distance, gathered around something. I couldn't really tell what it was, and as I got closer I saw that they were all looking up at something, but I still wasn't clear what it was. And as I got closer I could hear them applauding and saw there, in the middle of the crowd, a guy in a clown suit on stilts, juggling. And people were just ecstatic. It was as if Jesus had come back. They were climbing over each other to put money in his hat. I looked at the spectacle of it and thought, "It's a fuckin' clown, you know, do we need another fuckin' clown?" And then I kept walking down the street and about a block farther on another corner there was a guy playing saxophone. He was just standing there by himself and he was brilliant; he sounded like Coltrane, just blowing his guts out. Huge riffs. His neck looked like it was about to explode. No one was watching. There was like fifty cents in his sax case and a little stack of CDs. I looked up the street and saw a fresh crowd starting to gather around the juggling clown. Meanwhile, this guy's still blowing his guts out. Then he stops. I look at him and say, "Jesus, man, that was beautiful. Was that Coltrane?" He says, "No, it's an original, and if you like it so much, why don't you buy my fuckin' CD? It's on there."

"All right," I said. I pick up the CD and I look at it.

He says, "It's cut three." I turned over the CD. You know what it was called? It was called "Killing the Clown on Stilts."

At least that's how I read it.

After the show in D.C. I went back down to the strip bar, but I felt good this time. I thought it would make a difference in my experience of the club, but it didn't. There was a moment, though, that really moved me. It didn't happen when a dancer was dancing for me. After each dancer finished on the stage it was her job to wipe down the mirror behind her and the pole before the next dancer came up. I was thinking about how temporary disappointment can be if you don't linger on it too long and how there are beautiful things in the world if you look. It's up to you to find them for yourself. I looked up at my missing Vermeer, *Stripper Cleaning Mirror*.

11

The Clown and the Chair

The night I broke the orange chair was the night I realized my marriage to Mishna was really on the ropes. My rage transformed a piece of furniture into garbage and my wife into a terrified hostage. The final blow was when I told the story onstage.

Mishna and I had bought the chair on the street when we were furnishing our new house. There was a little white-haired man who sporadically sold used furniture out of a storage locker on Hollywood Boulevard near Western Avenue. There's a line of old garage doors that runs along the bottom of a building and sometimes he would be set up in front of an open one with his stuff out on the sidewalk. He was out there on Sundays, some Sundays.

We always rubbernecked his wares from the car. When we drove by he was always busy moving things around, rearranging. It seemed that there was an ever-evolving order to it all in his mind. He was a curator of the selected sellable detritus of other people's lives.

One day we were driving by and saw a clown painting on the

street. It looked like one of those classic old housewife hobby-painted clown heads in a cheesy wooden frame. We had to stop for the clown. We got out of the car and I walked quickly toward the painting, which was propped against the wall. I panic in yard sale and buffet situations. Even though there was no one else there looking at it I didn't want it to be snatched up. I always think I am going to miss out on a deal or some kind of food.

The painting was top-notch kitschy crap.

"Hello, excuse me. How much is this clown?" I asked the little man, who seemed to be looking for something in the garage.

He stopped rummaging and turned around. He looked confused and wise simultaneously, like a sweet cranky wizard or a midlevel hobbit.

"Oh, I don't know. It's a nice piece," he said, looking at it as if he had never really considered selling it. I wasn't clear whether that was his technique or his actual sentiment.

"I guess I can do one twenty-five."

"Seventy-five," my wife said.

He wrestled with the number on his face and did some hand scratching.

"Okay, one hundred," the wizard said.

"Sold!" I said preemptively, given my wife's look.

I was always impressed with her gumption but in that moment I fought it. I am not a good haggler. I don't like the game of it. I usually just pay what they ask for. I don't want to engage with the charade unless I don't care if I own what I am haggling for. There is a weird truth to the idea that if you really don't care, things will generally go your way. If you're really invested and emotionally attached, things will get away from you or at least get chaotic and scary. That's been my experience with relationships.

"You need anything else?" he asked, like we were putting him out. I began to wonder if he actually sold stuff or he just took the stuff out of the garage every so often to assess what he had.

"Yeah, we need a chair," I said.

He led us over to a beautiful modern Danish chair. It was curvy, with wooden sides and an orange leather seat and backrest. My wife loved it. It was going to be hers for her office in the house. It was probably from the forties, maybe the fifties; old but not fragile.

It shouldn't have broken as easily as it did.

"I love it," she said. "How much?"

"Uh, I don't know. It's the only one I have."

He seemed to want to hold on to everything we asked him about.

I said, "I'll give you one-fifty."

I shouldn't have started the negotiating. My wife gave me the "you should've let me handle this" look again.

"I don't know. That's a one of a kind. You know, I don't think I want to part with it."

I was pissed but I didn't care. I said, "Two hundred."

He said, "Yeah, okay, but take care of it. I've never seen one like that. It's a special chair."

"No problem," I snapped.

It seemed he really wanted his artifacts to be with the right people. I might have underestimated him at the time. He might have had a deeper understanding of the relationship between people and objects than the rest of us do. An odd pairing between a chair and a couple might disrupt the trajectory of the lives of the people and the chair. Of course, anything can be backloaded with meaning. That's how we explain things away when we don't want to take full responsibility for actions that are frightening and disastrous. It's the core of mysticism.

My wife was happy. She loved it. I was happy and felt like I had manned up to the moment. I had done it wrong but it still only cost me two hundred dollars.

"Anything else you're looking for? Or can I get on with my day?"

"We need curtains but I guess you don't really have that kind of stuff."

"I've got a lot more stuff that I haven't gone through. I do have some curtains but I don't know if they're for sale. Let's have a look."

The little man had kind of a hobble to his walk. We followed him to the garage locker door one down from the open one. He labored with a ring of keys and unlocked the white wooden doors and pulled them both open to reveal a massive mound of tables, chairs, lamps, paintings, and fabrics. Everything was piled on top of everything else. There was no way to walk around or check stuff out. It was a chaos mound of groovy treasure. My wife and I looked at each other like we had just been led into the cavern of cool truth.

We were excited, a secret stash. This all could have been part of his method. He lured curious people into his web of antique trash and made them feel like they were the first to lay eyes on the mid-century booty. As it turns out, the whole encounter became very mind-altering. I had no idea what was about to happen.

"I have some curtains up there. Can you see them?"

There was a huge unruly bundle of what looked to be the ugliest curtains in the world. My wife and I looked at each other.

"I don't know if those will work. Thanks for showing us," she said.

"Yeah, I don't think I can sell them."

Of course you don't, I thought.

"They were in Carl Jung's office," he said, flatly.

He must have seen me coming. He was an empath. He understood my uncapped personality, my propensity toward improvising the mystical, and hanging hope and power on inanimate objects.

"Carl Jung was in Los Angeles. How did I not know that?"

It seemed way too random to be bullshit. Suddenly, in my mind those curtains were an aperture for a room where a master sat doing the big work. The very mind that helped establish the fact that we are innately propelled toward something bigger than ourselves, and that spirituality is a primal deep craving based on universal archetypes that lay within the historical soul of the human experience. He invented the idea of the collective unconscious, for fuck's sake. He realized that synchronicity was real, in an almost magical way, relative to our perception, connections, and the power of meaning. I pictured him opening those curtains to let the day in, mandalas of pipe smoke surrounding him, as the great genius gazed out into the light.

"We have to have those curtains!" I blurted.

"They don't really fit the house," my wife said.

"Yeah, I'm not sure if I want to sell them."

The wizard decided I wasn't ready for the Jungian curtains. He was reluctant about the chair, too. Why was he judging me? What did he see within me? I was reading too much into it.

I paid the man. We loaded the chair and clown into the car and headed home.

I thought about those curtains for weeks. I thought about how they would change my life because they were saturated with unused Jung thoughts. I just needed to wring them out. Perhaps I could make a robe out of them, several robes. I could've created an entire line of Jungwear.

Then I did some research on Jung in L.A. Turns out it was highly unlikely that those curtains ever came in contact with the man. They were probably just in an office at the Jung Institute. I was disappointed and something died, maybe the dream of achieving a Jungian breakthrough via curtains.

I don't think those curtains could have stopped the emotional momentum of unmanaged cycles of primal rage in my marriage. I'm not sure anything could. Patterns had been set. My anger was unaddressed despite the damage it was causing. I just never thought it was a real problem, because when I was finished being angry I was done, every time. If you are a rager, when you are done raging you feel relief. It is out of you. It's like masturbating, only it's toxic to others and much harder to clean up. But even if the rager feels done, the rage will have generated in the other person a contempt that festers and swells, even if unspoken. Because the other person is afraid to speak.

The truth is that if you are ever yelling at a woman it doesn't matter what it is about because 95 percent of the time you should just be screaming, "Why can't you be my mommy? Why?" Or, "Why can't you be a better mommy than my mommy?" The other 5 percent is probably justified but there are other ways to communicate than yelling, I am told.

By the time the fight took place the orange chair was well established in my wife's office room. It had been over a year since we bought it. The clown had found its place on the wall in the bathroom. To this day when I look at myself in the mirror the sad clown is there looking down at me. That's as good a metaphor for my relationship with a god as I can come up with.

The reason for the fight was not specific. Once a fight starts it really doesn't matter what it is about, anyway. I know we were lying in bed. I was festering about something she hadn't done, or that she'd done, or that in my opinion she should have done, or that she might do if I didn't say something. I also knew we had made it through a day and I probably didn't need to say anything to fuck that up. Let me put it this way: There was absolutely no reason for me to say anything other than to start a fight. I was just one of those sick people who doesn't know if someone loves them unless the other person is crying. The fight began in my head.

Inner Good Marc: Hey, buddy, just let it go. It isn't worth it. So what? She did the thing that upsets you. It's really not that big a deal.

Inner Bad Marc: Shut up. I can't sleep. I thought I killed you in high school. I'm tired of being taken advantage of.

Inner Good Marc: You aren't. This is just one of those little things that really don't matter. She has to be able to do things. You can't control everything.

Inner Bad Marc: You're a pussy. This is important. She disrespects me all the time and it keeps happening.

Inner Good Marc: Disrespect is a bit much. Maybe she just doesn't know how to communicate with you because you are so pissed-off all the time and she does covert things to get back at you for stifling her.

Inner Bad Marc: Exactly. That's why I'm going to bring it up!

(Marc exits his head and enters the bed. His wife is falling asleep.)

Marc: Hey, baby. Why did you do that thing today?

Marc's Wife: What thing?

Marc: You know, that thing that pisses me off because it's rude.

Marc's Wife: I don't want to do this right now.

Marc: Do what? We're having a conversation.

Marc's Wife: No, we're not. You are starting a fight and I don't want to cry tonight. I want to go to sleep.

Marc: I just don't understand why you did that thing. You keep doing it.

Marc's Wife: (getting out of bed) I don't want to do this again. (She goes into her office room, slams the door, and starts dressing.) I'm leaving.

Marc: (following her, aggressively pushing door open) Wait. I just wanted to talk about it.

Marc's Wife: No, you didn't. I just want to leave. Please let me leave. I don't want to do this anymore.

Marc: Wait, don't leave.

Marc's Wife: Please let me leave. (She starts crying.)

Marc: No, don't leave. What do you mean leave? For how long? Why?

Marc's Wife: (Hysterical) Just let me leave.

(Marc picks up the orange chair like he is going to move it. Lifts it a foot off the ground and slams it on the floor for effect. The chair, in an almost cartoonlike way, falls apart in three pieces. First one side, then the other, then the center falls out. Marc's wife is crying hysterically.)

Marc's Wife: You're breaking things. It's not safe. I'm leaving. I'm leaving.

Marc: What are you talking about? It broke itself. What a piece of shit. You could've hurt yourself on this thing.

(She makes a run for the front door. Marc stops her. Grabs her arms. Looks at her.)

Marc: Please don't leave.

(He sees for the first time she is terrified and doesn't like him at all. His heart drops. He has gone too far.)

Marc: I'll leave. I should leave.

(Marc prepares to leave.)

My wife sat down on the couch. Crying. I floundered around. Trying to worm out of leaving. I knew that I should be the one to leave. I am the man. I fucked up. I didn't want to run her out of the house but I also didn't want her to leave because I didn't know if or when she would come back and I couldn't live with that. I thought I had control over that. That is the core of emotional abuse.

"You want me to leave?"

She looked exhausted and destroyed.

"Can't we just get past this?"

She wasn't talking. Despondent.

"Okay, I guess I'm leaving. It's one in the morning. Are you sure you want me to go?"

I started to collect my things. Keys, I put my jacket on, I opened the door.

"Shit, toothbrush." I turned around to go back in the house. She stood up from the couch and with an intensity and focus of anger I had never seen from her before said, "Just get the fuck out."

I did. She slammed the door behind me.

I get in my car. It's one-thirty in the morning, I'm in Los Angeles, and I don't know where I'm going to go. I'm scared and crazy. My first thought is, "I don't know any hotels. Maybe I'll just go downtown and go to the Standard. That's nice. Maybe they put a little mint on the pillow. Take a swim tomorrow. Maybe I'll get a good breakfast." Then there is that part of me that thinks, "Marc, this is a dark night of the soul. You have to go to a dark night of the soul hotel."

I decide that is the way to go: sleazy and self-punishing. I drive around the shitty part of L.A. where I live and I find this crappy hotel. It's weird. It's got bulletproof glass where you get your key and pay for the room in advance.

There's a couple of transvestite hookers there. I'm walking up to my room thinking, "Well, this is it. It's the dark night of the soul." One of the tranny hookers says, "Hey, you wanna date?"

I find something compelling about them for reasons I don't understand but my plate is a little full and I decide it isn't the night to wade into these waters.

"No, thanks," I say, slightly frightened of myself.

The room is just a shitty hotel room. Two shitty beds. Wood paneling. A TV with no cable. It's hard to have a dark night of the soul when you don't drink or do drugs or fuck trannies. The drama is limited. I just sit there rocking on the end of the bed talking to myself and crying.

"Fuck her! Maybe not! I dunno! Maybe it's me!"

I'm just in there weeping on a shitty bed with two channels of

TV thinking maybe I should get one of those trannies in here and talk to her. I don't know what I would have said.

"Well, you seem to have worked shit out. You've made some pretty dramatic decisions for your own wholeness. Can you help me?"

I don't. I just sit there. I don't sleep. I cry. I watch the clock, wondering when it will officially be a whole night. When?

When the sun comes up I decide it's official, a night has passed. It's 5:30 A.M. I'm going back. I drive back to my house in the cutting light of an up-all-night morning. I pull up my street to see she's already put the chair out in front of the house. It sits there barely put together like a shame throne. An example to the rest of the neighborhood. I feel like Lance Kerwin in that movie *The Loneliest Runner* from when I was a kid. He was a bed wetter and he learned to run because his mom would put out his piss-stained sheets for all to see and he'd have to run home before his friends saw them and pull them down.

I park the car and scurry over to the chair, pick it up, hold it together, and run it into the backyard. It isn't garbage day. It is already bad enough that I am sure that the entire neighborhood has heard us fighting all the time. When I would run into my neighbors while putting out our garbage I would fight the urge to say, "Hey, I'm not hitting her."

I knock. I think it was my feeble attempt at showing respect and having boundaries. My wife opens the door. I walk in.

"Hi. Sorry. Are we going to be okay?"

I am weepy and contrite. It is predictable at this point. She is detached.

"I really don't know."

"Damnit!"

There is nothing worse than the feeling that you have lost your love and she is standing right in front of you.

"Maybe we should go to couples counseling."

She had suggested this many times before and I just pushed it off into the future. Well, the future was here and it was too late. We went but at that point it was really an ambush that I paid for. I paid someone three hundred dollars to watch my wife call me an asshole for an hour. I sat there and said, "I know. I know! I acted like an asshole. Asshole. Wait, now. What about you?" I had no right to that question by the time we got there, according to her.

Soon after this turning point I was invited to perform at the Aspen Comedy Festival to be part of an event featuring the Moth, a New York–based storytelling group. The theme was "On Thin Ice." So I thought there was no better tale to tell than that of the breaking of the chair. I mean, I was on thin ice, no doubt. Our anniversary also fell on one of the dates we were there. I made dinner plans and my wife said I shouldn't worry about it, that we didn't have to go out and make a big deal about it. I'm pretty sure now that she was already emotionally involved with another man and she was just stringing me along getting her ducks in a row.

I'm about to do the Moth show and I'm freaking out because I'm not sure what story to tell.

"I don't know what story to tell," I said. My best thinking at the time led me to ask her this: "Hey, would you mind if I told the story about the chair? Breaking the chair? It's a good story."

She said, "I don't care, Marc."

"No, seriously. I'm asking your permission because it's pretty hairy. I'll make sure I look like the asshole because I was the asshole. I'll make that clear. It's funny, it's deep, it's real, it's fucking awful."

"Do what you want."

"Okay. You sure? You cool? Because I can do a cat thing."

"No. Do the chair story. That will be good."

I think she was either unconsciously or maybe intentionally setting me up to do as much stupid shit as possible so she could make an undeniable case for herself to leave me. Despite how I make myself look, here I tried to give her whatever she wanted. I tried to love her properly but I was incapable and scared. I was obsessed with her leaving to such a degree that I made it happen. I didn't take responsibility for my anger and it sank me. All I really wanted for her was to be successful and realize her dreams. Which she did, after she left me.

It was an odd show. Billy Baldwin was also performing. The Aspen Comedy Festival was a prestigious event. Everyone from the comedy industry was there. It was sponsored by HBO. I get onstage in front of everybody in show business and I tell the story. I stand before almost every one of our peers, most of the comedy industry, and say, "I'm an emotionally abusive douche bag and she's the one I fucking make cry all the time." Billy Baldwin came up to me after the show and said, "You don't deserve her."

If a Baldwin is giving me relationship advice I must be pretty far gone. I get offstage, I look at my wife, and she's upset, she's crying, she's livid.

"What do you think this makes me look like?" she sputtered out as soon as I reached her.

"Well, I asked you!"

"Goddamnit, Marc!"

"What do you mean?"

"I'm embarrassed. You made a fool of me in front of all these people."

I didn't see it that way. I thought if I could frame it as a story, as a piece of comedy with me as the butt of the joke, I would be absolved in her eyes. I thought that publicly showing my faults and my desire to change would work. I also thought if I could make this horror story funny it would be a profound example of what I could do as a comic. This is the risk of living your art. If your life is disintegrating, saying so publicly doesn't necessarily reverse the rot. Usually the opposite is true, especially if the bit works.

When we get back to the hotel room she's completely detached. I can't sleep. I feel bad and I have to do a political panel show in the morning. I fall asleep for a second and I have this horrible dream. It isn't a narrative dream, more of a feeling. There is a setting but it is uneventful: I'm outside, the sky is gray. There are no mandalas unless they are hiding in a vague cloud of terror. All I know is that I am alone. That is all the dream was. The realization that I am alone. I wake up and say, "I can't . . . I can't sleep. I'm freakin' out, baby. Baby, baby . . ."

Waking up she says, "What? What do you want? I have a ski race tomorrow."

"Well, I'm fucking losin' it."

"Yeah, so what's new?"

"Well, can we just talk? Help me out!"

"You want me to blow you?"

"Okay."

I knew that would take my mind off the end of my marriage and the stress of the show. She was angry and I think in her mind blowing me would be easier than talking to me. Have you ever had a spiteful, detached blowjob? Have you ever had one that had the subtext of *this is it*. Not a happy ending. She avoided me the entire next day.

We get back from Aspen. Obviously it's strained and stressed. I didn't know she was moving toward somebody else. I don't know what's going on. All I know is that there's not a lot of fucking going on. There are other forms of sex, but not fucking. Hand jobs were never my bag. To me they're a struggle. I can do that myself. But all of a sudden she's decided, "I just want to do that now."

"Really?"

She was presenting it like it was a great option, her new thing. In retrospect what she was telling me was, "That thing you've got there is not going anywhere near my vagina ever again. This arm's length is the distance that will always exist, between that thing and me. This is as far as it goes."

It was completely naïve and insensitive of me not to realize how far away my behavior had forced her. It really wasn't until I came back from a week's work in New York and she left me that I really got it. It was about a month after the Aspen festival. I had been out doing shows with Henry Rollins and Janeane Garofalo. My wife picked me up at LAX, gave me a bottle of water, and drove me home. During the ride I was telling her about the show. She seemed detached but that wasn't unusual by that point. In the middle of that ride from the airport, out of nowhere, my wife said, "Marc, you really are a genius." Her tone was odd and the sentiment seemed to come out of nowhere. Unsolicited. Usually a statement like that is preceded by me pacing around beating the shit out of myself, yelling, "I'm a fraud! I am a fucking loser!" But this came out of nowhere in a dead voice and for no reason.

"Thanks," I said. "Why did you say that?"

"Because you are."

We got to the house and walked in. I put my bags down and she went into the kitchen, sat at the table, and started crying. I walked into the kitchen and said, "What's wrong?"

"I want a trial separation," she said.

"Why?" I said.

I knew why. I didn't know what else to say. It was just an impulse to dialogue. When I heard her speak and I looked at her face it was clear that she was done and was now pleading for some kind of permission from herself. Not me. I watched her walk out with no luggage and I said, "What am I supposed to do?" She said, "I don't know. Call someone."

That was it.

Months later, after it became apparent that she wasn't coming back, I entered some kind of post-traumatic stress syndrome. Everything was emotionally heightened and dead simultaneously. It was confusing and exhausting. I was a functioning catatonic on fire on the inside. I was surrounded by a haze of pain.

I was driving home one afternoon during this period when I rolled past a woman putting household objects and furniture out in her front yard. I figured it was a garage sale or she was termite bombing. As I moved past her house an object I saw stopped me. Dragged me into the present. A chair. The chair? The orange Danish modern chair that I broke and that subsequently broke up my marriage appeared to be sitting on her front lawn. "Impossible," I thought. That was destroyed, thrown out, gone. I stopped my car abruptly in the street, opened my car door, and ran up into her yard. She was pulling more stuff out of her house. I said, "Hi. Hey, are you selling this stuff?"

"Just take whatever you want. I'm leaving," she said, going angrily about her business.

"Where did you get this chair? I used to have one exactly like it. I've never seen another one."

"I found it," she said. "Take it."

I inspected the chair. It had been carefully rebuilt, put back together. It was the chair.

"Did you find this on the street up on the hill around the corner?"

"Yeah," she said. "Why?"

"This chair destroyed my marriage."

She looked at me with a dark, stressed gaze for a second like she was looking through me at something burning in the distance and said, "Mine, too."

I didn't ask any questions. Synchronicity was upon us. The causality was there, it was explainable, but the meaning of the object before us was at once unique and shared. It was some kind of black magic that sent my thoughts back to the garage wizard who kept Jung's curtains locked up. What had he unleashed on this world, my world, her world, with this chair?

"We have to take it out of circulation."

"Yes," she said, catatonically, like how I felt.

Then this stranger and I proceeded to destroy the chair with our hands and our feet until it was unfixable. We took a breath and looked down at the scattered chair shards.

"Thanks," she said.

A horn honked. I turned to see my car, door open, sitting in the middle of the street, running. Someone needed to get by.

"Good luck with everything," I said, then walked back to my car and drove away, strangely relieved. I glanced in my rearview mirror and saw her making a pile of culprit pieces.

★ Part II ★

NORMAL

WTF #269

April 9, 2012

Marc: Do you find it weird that as we get older, there's this whole element of, like, *Wait, what happened to that guy?* You know what I mean?

David Cross: Yeah, of course.

M: And it's very hard for me to frame it because I see points in my life where I'm like, *I could be that guy.* And I have a tremendous heavy heart about it. You know, when you run into people and you're like, *Hey, what have you been doing?* and they are like, *Well . . . uh . . . I don't know.* Isn't there something heartbreaking about the whole thing?

D: Yeah . . . depending on the person, depending on the path they took and what they did along that path. I mean, I think you're as good an example as anybody because you were clearly gifted and talented, and you also had a lot of demons, and you exacerbated the situation irresponsibly [*laughing*] and then you got to a point . . . and you were still able to kind of power through, but you had also sort of plateaued at that point.

M: Yeah.

D: And I don't know what it was that motivated you, um, nor do I care to know.

M: Yeah. [*Laughing*]

D: But you eventually cleaned up. And you're a better person for it; you're a better comedian; you're a better writer. There are people who didn't do that.

★ **Chapter 12** ★

Babies

I've had two wives but no children. When my first wife started reading baby books, that was a red flag to me and I freaked out. I knew I had to get out. I wasn't ready. I felt like if I had kids I would have no life. That everything I wanted to accomplish would have to go on hold or get ditched to service the kid. That my ridiculous show business dream would have to be reined in and I would just have to do whatever was necessary to support a family. That I would be resigned to a life of bitter surrender, trying not to infect the kid with my sadness and disappointment, hoping that the kid didn't notice my deep resentment of his or her part in my failure.

So, clearly, I wasn't in the right frame of mind.

When I was with the second wife I thought maybe we could do it. Maybe we should do it. In my mind, I was ready. She wasn't. She put it very succinctly: "You think I'm going to bring children into this?" My response was something along the lines of, "What does that even fucking mean? You don't think I'd be a good father? Fuck you. Fuck this." The fact is, she was right. I was an abusive, selfish, needy, angry asshole.

Now I'm just kind of selfish, a little less angry, occasionally needy, with flights of asshole. I've grown.

After the second divorce I accepted that I wouldn't have kids. I didn't have a woman in my life. I was getting old. I would probably be happier without them. I could put an end to the genetic bundle of selfishness, depression, and anger that has tumbled down through time along my father's line of descent. I would be doing the world a favor.

I'm not sure my parents even wanted to have kids. I think they did it because that was what they were supposed to do; it was what their generation *did*. The truth is, they were kids themselves when they had me. My mother was twenty-two and my father was twenty-six. I don't really think of them as parents. They're just these people I grew up with who were a little older than me. My parents were always too worried and panicky, too consumed with themselves to ever make me feel like things would be okay. So now I'm a panicky, worried, self-consumed adult who is fundamentally unable to feel like things will be okay. There is some part of me that will always be looking, futilely, for a parent to just make things okay.

My mother has stepped up her parenting game over the last few years, and she applies these new skills to my brother Craig's three kids. Grandkids have given her a second shot at being a parent, but in a more hands-off situation. She seems to be excelling.

But when I watch my father around Craig's kids, it makes me sad to think of little me being raised by this man. He engages with them for a few minutes, until he realizes they aren't really all that interested in him. Then he detaches. I was in Phoenix for the bat mitzvah of one of Craig's kids and I had to go pick my father up at his hotel and bring him over to the house. I got to the hotel and I said to my father, "You ready to go?"

"Where we going?" he asked. He was getting dressed.

"We're going over to Craig's so you can hang out with the grandkids, right?"

Without irony or a second thought my father said, "Yeah, you know, some people get something out of that. I don't get anything out of that." Completely deadpan.

So I said, "Well, what do want to do?"

"You remember those mustard slacks I had? You can't find those anymore. I've looked all over."

"Okay," I said, a little afraid of the non sequitur.

"Let's go across the street to the mall and see if they've got them."

My father and I then went to the mall across the street, where he walked into the most expensive store he could find and dropped three hundred dollars on a pair of almost-mustard slacks. Then we went to my niece's bat mitzvah brunch so my father could show off his pants.

I am at a crossroads. I am in a relationship with a women who is twenty years younger than I am. I'm not bragging. The age difference presents its own set of problems but I love her. When we met we had no idea that we would end up together. We thought we were just going to hang out, have fun, and move on. Now, after three years of very intense trials and tribulations, fits and starts, we are living together and she wants a baby. I know this because she says things like, "When are you going to put a baby in me?" I'm thinking, "I don't know. When you frame it differently?"

I knew this was something she always wanted and now I find myself thinking, "Well, if I'm going to do it, it's going to have to be with someone her age, and I love her. This is it. This is when it will happen."

Now it is pressing. Everything within her is screaming *baby now*. When she's not worrying about her own years of fertility, she's concerned that if we wait much longer I will be too old to make it for the long haul as a father. She's worried that by the time it all shakes out, she will have wasted years on me.

I'm afraid that I'm already too old. When I tell people that, they say, "You're a guy. You can have kids until you're a hundred if you still have cum in your balls and a way to get it out." Sorry, didn't mean to get clinical.

In response to that I say, "I don't want to do that to a kid."

I remember the first kid I met with an old dad. It might have been in nursery school. I can't remember the kid's name but I recall waiting around after school for our parents to show up. Eventually some old guy pulled up in a car and got out. I said to the kid, "Who's that?"

"That's my dad."

"How old is he?"

"I don't even know."

"Does he do anything?"

"Yeah, sometimes. I gotta go. I have to help him."

I don't want a kid to go through that. It has been pointed out to me by people with old dads that your dad is your dad and that's it. You love him regardless. That sounds good in theory. I'm not quite sold.

I know it's trendy for a man in his late forties or fifties to have his first kid after a life of self-indulgence and fun craps out on him and doesn't deliver the deep win with the lasting answers. I don't want to be that guy.

On the other hand, I see men in their fifties and sixties who have never had kids and I feel that they are missing something, some wisdom, some fundamental humility that comes with being forced to reckon with the kind of responsibility and selflessness that can only come from taking care of a child.

Except for George Clooney. He seems okay.

Maybe I'm projecting. I'm sure I am. That is how I glean meaning. I make up lives and vibes for people I meet and see.

The woman I'm with would be a great mother. She works with severely emotionally disturbed and autistic children. She teaches kids in very difficult situations how to relax and communicate. The patience necessary for that task is daunting and impressive. That on top of the patience necessary to deal with my bullshit should earn this woman some kind of humanitarian award. Or a child.

Why can't I just do it? Just make a baby? I'm terrified. When she brings it up I hear it as an attack or an ultimatum. I hear it as a manipulation, a trap, a way of staying connected to me, keeping me tethered to her for the rest of my life. My brain spins fear scenarios. Here's the list.

1. The baby will be born dead.
2. The baby will die.
3. She will eventually hate me and turn the baby against me.
4. I won't know how to do the baby thing.
5. I won't be able to afford the baby thing.
6. The baby won't like me.
7. I will drop the baby.
8. I will ruin the baby.

9. I will not be alive when the baby grows up.

10. She will take my baby and go live with another man.

We argue about it all the time. The arguments become horrible and full of anger and pain. She wants it to be fun, exciting, a new life, a family. I am buzzkilling her very real and reasonable wants and it breaks my heart. We've been going to couples counseling to get me in the baby zone. To figure out what my fear is and overcome it. I love kids, I get along with kids, they seem to like me. What has been holding me back? People who have babies tell me I will know a love that is beyond anything I can imagine, and a joy that is indescribable. Love and joy? That sounds horrifying. I have no way of knowing whether I can handle either of those. I'm much better with need and fear. They are what ground me.

I still need someone in my life to make me feel like things will be okay.

All day every day I go back and forth. I drift into a fantasy of the amazing life I'd have with a baby, immersed in the all-consuming but rewarding work of raising a child. Then moments later, for no good reason, I see the exact same scenario as being a hell on earth with no way out, full of drama, heartache, and pain. This is the cycle that spins daily in my head.

Then there's the weekly cycle: Every week she brings up the fact that she wants a baby, a new house, and an engagement ring. That's the panic trifecta for me. I usually spiral into a diplomatic but evasive argument about the struggle I'm having making the decision on at least two of the topics at hand. That gets her angry because she doesn't understand why she is with a man who isn't excited about doing those things with her. I make my case: I'm old, twice divorced, and emotionally retarded. She cries. I get mad that we are having the discussion again and try to bolster my defense with the fact that we are "working on it" in therapy.

The other night the argument began when we were in bed. Bedtime is the worst time to start an argument because all the drama unfolds while you are wearing your underwear. Being angry in your underwear is a hard thing to pull off. We had reached the moment that pitches me over the edge into rage. I found myself standing beside my bed in boxers screaming with embarrassing intensity, "I hate you. I hate you. I hate you!"

And I stomped out of the room and down the hall and stood in the living room for a few seconds. Then I walked back down the hall, back into the bedroom, and sat on the bed still fuming.

She said, "Breathe, breathe, breathe."

I had a tantrum. I am a child.

I took a deep breath. Then another. Then I started weeping.

"It's okay to be sad. You're going to be okay," she said, touching my shoulder.

"I love you. I'm sorry," I said, whimpering.

"I love you too," she said, comforting me, sternly. "But I'm not going to hang around forever."

★ 13 ★

Viagra Diaries

I don't like porn. I use it occasionally but I don't like it. It is disturbing how pornified this culture has become and how integrated it is in our lives. It's almost hard to avoid it. I think that some computers actually have porn on them when you buy them. You boot it up and bam, there are two people fucking on your desktop.

I saw porn way too young. It permanently twisted my mind up about what was expected out of me sexually. I can clearly remember my first photographic porn image. It was a woman sucking a cock, holding it, cum coming out of her mouth and down the shaft, all over her hands, her face angled up at a guy with a Van Dyke facial hair configuration, his eyes closed and mouth gaping. That picture seared itself into my brain more than any piece of art I'd seen or anything from life itself, for that matter, for years. It didn't begin to fade until I put more porn in my brain.

If I were a fifteen-year-old boy living in this culture today I would never leave my room. My head would explode from masturbating so much. I would have worn my cock to a nub. When I was a kid it was hard to find porn. We didn't have the Internet. You had to know the guy with the weird brother or the dad that had a stash and that was usually soft-core stuff. Or you had to find that one page of a hard-core mag under a bridge somewhere with your friends. All of you looking at first confused but then suddenly enlightened, fighting over who gets to take it home first.

"I feel funny in my pants. I'm taking it first."

Then you'd all go back every day under that bridge for a month to see if the rest of the magazine magically appeared, as if there were porn trolls out distributing loose pages of hard-core fucking in the middle of the night. Little hordes of warty slobbering grunting half-demons.

"We must put out more filth for the children. They must learn somewhere. I'll get the bridge. You guys get the gas station bathrooms and behind the dumpsters."

I realize now that there really were porn trolls. They were people who would go jerk off in strange locations because they had nowhere else to go. They needed a secret place. The forgotten pages were memorials to the marginalized life of the sexual deviant, the man who had to masturbate outdoors, under bridges.

I know this to be true because of something I saw in Boston when I was in college. I was walking across the highway bridge just outside Kenmore Square. The bridge comes off Beacon Street and spans a runoff ditch of some kind. There are actually two bridges, one for each direction. It was late morning and I was hungover. I was on one of the bridges, looking down into the dirty water and the underpass of the other bridge, when I saw two sets of legs hanging over a ledge. One set of legs was human and had pants around its ankles and the other set of legs was inflatable and dangling. It was like a dirty cartoon. I watched for a few seconds before both sets of appendages disappeared up into the dark side of the underpass. Some guy, out of what necessity or what desire I don't know, was fucking a blowup doll under a bridge in the middle of the day. I didn't know what to do with that. I certainly thought it was a ballsy way to spend the morning.

I have nothing morally against porn but it is dangerous to let in your head, for a few reasons. Even though I didn't understand how it actually worked, I was completely obsessed with sex from about age ten. All I could think about was naked women all the time. Any women. Naked. Good. The first time I masturbated was an accident. I stuck my cock into the water running out of the bath faucet and it changed my life. It took me a while to stop fucking water and move to my hand but the transition was made and it became and remains a regular activity.

The first time I saw the mechanics of intercourse illustrated was actually in the aisle of a B. Dalton Bookseller in the Winrock Center mall in Albuquerque, New Mexico, where I grew up. I must've been eleven or twelve. I was in the humor section looking through *The History of Underground Comics*. There was a panel done by Spain Rodriguez of two people fucking in outer space as if they were part of the galaxy, a constellation. It was there I saw how the penis went into the vagina. I also saw it in R. Crumb's panels. I now knew how it all fit together. The feeling of looking at that for the first time, the body rush, the flow of blood to both heads, the exploding virgin brain figuring out one of the few known keys to the universe, can never be recaptured. Masturbation now had visual definition and structure. It was one of the best moments of my life. I guess it's a bit telling that I almost came in my pants in what was basically the joke book section of a bookstore, but I didn't. I went and jerked off in the mall bathroom instead. I had no choice in that moment. I guess if you hold on to that innocent, youthful combination of overwhelming desire and unstoppable need for release, there is no reason you wouldn't find yourself under a bridge fucking a doll.

Seeing my first porn movie was devastating in terms of the

damage it did to my brain. I have a love-hate relationship with porn. As I said, I use it. I obviously like it. I know it isn't good for my brain, my life, my relationships, or my sexual sensitivity but I watch it because it's a drug that is free and the only paraphernalia I need to get high is already hanging off of my body, an arm's length away at all times.

I saw a few great seventies porns when I was in my early teens. In this order: *Deep Throat, The Opening of Misty Beethoven,* and *The Rites of Uranus.* The first two I saw were on Betamax video. My parents had borrowed them from a couple that they were friendly with. The woman of that couple was stunning and now I knew she was also nasty. My fourteen-year-old brain ran with that and calloused my paraphernalia. The fact that my mother told me that my parents had porn and where they got it and that it was hidden somewhere in the house is certainly dubious in its appropriateness, but boundaries are for normal families. My family functioned as a singular emotionally amoebic unit, all of us in search of primordial union.

The Rites of Uranus really set a bad table of expectations for me. I must've been about fifteen. My friends and I all got drunk and took our fake IDs to this porno theater. I don't remember what the movie was about but I do know a guy showed up in a town on a bus, met a girl, and they ended up in bed fucking. She had a tattoo of the devil on her stomach, with her vagina and pubic hair forming his mouth and beard. She kept shouting, "Fuck me, fuck the devil! Fuck me, fuck the devil!"

It's rough to be a virgin and have a vagina be the mouth of Satan in your mind before you have even dealt with a real one. In retrospect, I'm not sure it's not a fitting metaphor for some vaginas. You can lose your house and all your money to a really hungry one.

Outside of blowing my mind and turning me into a masturbating fiend, the pornos were a template in my brain of how sex was done. I hadn't done it yet but I knew what was expected. I was supposed to have a huge, hard cock that could fuck for what seemed like hours, then I came somewhere outside of the vagina onto a woman's body. I thought this was how all guys were, hard at the drop of a dime and able to fuck forever if necessary. It was all I knew at the time and what I struggle with today. It's typical of how I've developed my sense of self. I have had to cobble it together on my own because my parents never cut me loose, because of their own fears and needs, but they never guided me in any way, either. They just sort of let me flounder to figure it out on my own. Which is its own kind of freedom, but your sources may be suspect.

I brought all my porn-derived sexual wisdom to my first few sexual encounters but my dick never made it out of my pants. It just did what it had to do all by itself without me even touching it. Just by grinding into the crotch of a girl. I never saw this in porn so I was pretty sure I was screwed up somehow, and I became incredibly scared I would never fuck in earnest.

As it turns out, coming in my pants would be a lot less stressful than actual sex.

The first few times I had actual sex, the experience was trying and messy. I imagine that's somewhat par for the real-world course but the course I was on was the porno course and I was failing. I lost my virginity when I was seventeen to a waitress at the restaurant I was working at. The place was right across from the University of New Mexico and all the waitresses were in college or older. The owner was a manic Jewish blow monkey named Eddie, from Brooklyn. Eddie was obsessed with the fact that I was a virgin, a fact I'd revealed over a few lines of coke. He then secretly offered all the waitresses money to deflower me. There was a bounty on my virginity, although I didn't know this till after the fact.

The woman who took the bait (I don't know if she was ever paid) was named Cheryl. She was twenty-seven or so, slightly heavy, hippieish but very cool and charming. She had a similar personality to Diane Keaton in *Annie Hall*. She came up to me during a morning shift and said, "Come over this afternoon at four-thirty and bring champagne." So I had all day to freak out. Most guys would have been thrilled but I was filled with panic. All I had in my head was porn. I had a performance anxiety monster that lived within me and grabbed my balls from the inside every time I came close to having actual sex.

I got to her place at four-thirty sharp. She got undressed and we went right to it. It was unruly. She had big, never-been-disciplined hippie-girl boobs and a massive mound of hair on her pussy. That was normal back then. Now you never see that. Then if you saw a shaved pussy you would've thought it had cancer. So, once I got it up and in it was over in about twelve seconds. Probably not an unusual event but I immediately started beating myself up in front of her. She was supportive but there was no way she could've spun it into a victory. I left, apologies abounding. Which would be the title of a memoir I could write about all of my sexual exploits, at least all of them before I met my first real girlfriend when I was nineteen.

Samantha was a punk rock girl who ate at the same dining hall as me in college. I was an aspiring pseudo-intellectual who wrote plays, acted, wore round glasses, and dressed in secondhand overcoats. You know the guy. That was me. She had dyed red hair and a shaved patch over her left ear. I just wanted her. It came from that strange combination of contempt and curiosity. Who the fuck does she think she is? That haircut is bullshit. What is she really like? I want that.

I started to perceive my obsession as love and put a lot of energy into following through on it. I was persistent, charming, intense, and prone to writing poetry if necessary. Turned out she had just gotten out of a relationship with a woman and had a long sexual history going back to high school and a guitar player. I was completely threatened but focused. I would make her straight and erase the licks of her old boyfriend with my chaotic Jewish neediness, anger, and hypersensuality.

Well, I got her and thankfully learned how to fuck semi-well. I had a lot to prove. I was a half-impotent premature ejaculator who was now representing my gender with a bisexual woman who was fresh out of a lesbian relationship. I was not open-minded at the time. I just wanted to win. I learned the nuances of vaginas and how to treat them with my mouth. I figured out that when I make someone else come it turns me on more than anything so I started doing that first. In retrospect I think I was just covering my bases preemptively. Get her off at least once, then the pressure is off. It was touch-and-go but it certainly changed my life. Finally I knew the basics of actually having sex. I also learned that I was insanely possessive, insecure, jealous, and controlling. In other words she eventually ran away with me screaming behind her. She kept running till she was in another country.

That was the first heartbreak and I really got into it. I started drinking heavily. I decided my identity would revolve around booze, coke, anger, and fucking. So, that's what I did. During that period I met Lisa the welder. She was amazing. I was drunk at a Steve Albini show at the Rathskeller in Kenmore Square. She was this tank of a girl in the crowd. Short, curvy, black jeans, and a big black Mohawk. She was sexually menacing, bordering on scary. I needed to have her.

We left the club and went to her house. She was an art student whose medium was metal. In her bedroom was a large emaciated female figure made out of welded steel, with a gaping vagina full of actual nails. How I didn't read that as a sign to split I don't know. Instead I was completely taken with her and we embarked on a drunken journey to the heart of angry sex. I loved her but I couldn't handle her.

Lisa filled in a large gap in my sexual education. Due to some abuse issues she was incapable of having an orgasm but she loved to fuck, for a long time, to make up for what she was missing in the orgasm department. I was not used to being unable to make a woman have an orgasm or to fucking for a long time. If I didn't last as long as Lisa wanted she would get angry and her anger was scary. This is why I learned to fuck without coming: Lisa on top of me, looking me straight in the eyes, saying, "Don't you fucking come. Don't do it. I'm not done. Don't fucking come."

I was scared. Out of practicality and fear I had to learn how to have sex for as long as necessary. Once when she got worried I was going to come too quickly she wrapped a fake pearl necklace around my dick to the point of constriction and pain and sat on it and told me to wait to come until she was done. That did the trick. Lisa and I ended in booze, yelling, betrayal, a trip to Carlsbad Caverns in a rented Delta 88, and sadness.

With Samantha I was told by a girl who likes girls that I gave the best head, and I learned that turning someone else on is actually the biggest turn-on. With Lisa I learned a lifelong respect for truly creative women who can't help but honor their imagination and I learned how to fuck for a long time. I'm still in touch with both of them. Lots of water under the bridge, and luckily I'm not under there with it fucking a blowup lady.

I have told these stories to somehow establish the unreasonable but maybe not uncommon importance I put on sex as something that defines me and my relationships. I worked hard at becoming good at it, probably harder than anything in my life other than comedy. Intimacy, trust, commitment, and all the other ideas and qualities that define a good relationship fell by the wayside while I was developing my sex juggernaut. I'm not bragging. I've realized that it's shallow to allow sex to define a relationship or to think that good sex will save it when the chips are down. It will not. Which brings us to Viagra.

When my second wife left me I was a broken man on all levels, from the top floor to the subbasement where I kept all my childhood embarrassments. It crushed me. I was left feeling like a slug, incapable of charm, and even my anger had wilted to sadness. In other words, I was not feeling sexy. Still, I didn't want to let my health go, so I made it a point to make my yearly physical. I have two doctors, one on each coast. I have Dr. Murray Heichman on the west coast, Dr. Jacob Metzger on the east. I only let old Jewish men finger-bang me. I had a bad experience with a young Asian doctor once. I don't think it has anything to do with him being Asian.

I went to the Asian doctor that one time because I had changed insurance plans and he was the guy at the place. Prostate exams are obviously a vulnerable and uncomfortable situation, but you know it's part of the gig. So I was bent over the examination table with my pants and my underwear pulled down. This new doctor put his finger in me. There are moments in life when you realize that your prostate might be fun, sexually speaking. The examination table with your doctor's finger up your ass isn't the right place for that realization. In the middle of the process, finger in my ass, this young Asian doctor in a slight accent of some kind says, "Oooh, smooth."

I didn't know what it meant. Was that good? Bad? Was it necessary for him to say that during the examination? I didn't think so. As a doctor you should wait until you're washing up to expound on the condition of the gland. Just saying "smooth" in the middle of the awkwardness gave me no other recourse but to turn my head around in slight panic and say, "Is that good? Am I okay?" Those words, spoken in that position, can only be humiliating. As he exited his finger from my ass he said, "Smooth, good."

Having a prostate exam brings up some old weird memories around race and ass exams in general. These are memories from the subbasement. When I was ten my family moved to Albuquerque, New Mexico, from Anchorage, Alaska. My father was in the air force. He did his two years in Alaska and started his medical practice in New Mexico. We had been there maybe a few weeks when I started having bad abdominal pains, which in retrospect were probably just gas. What I went through for that gas was horrible. My father is and was both an overreactive hypochondriac and a physician, which is a bad combination. There were a lot of unorthodox examinations in the house, unorthodox in the sense that they were done at the house. I don't think they were necessarily inappropriate procedures, but I do wonder. He was an orthopedic surgeon. He didn't know everything.

When I had these pains my father decided to give me a rectal exam to determine whether I had appendicitis. He was a doctor and my dad and I was ten. I rode it out. It was uncomfortable but as the child of a physician there were times when you had to make that separation between dad and doctor. If your dad is finger-banging you in the bathroom, that is a bad thing. If a doctor is finger-banging you to determine whether you are sick, that is an appropriate thing. When the finger-banging is being done by your dad the doctor in the bathroom of your own house, lines start to feel a little blurred. On a lighter note, in these moments I had my father's undivided attention, which was usually hard to come by.

Given that my father was not an internist, his examination yielded nothing that he could accurately diagnose. He then called the only other doctor he knew in this new town. Dr. Chester came over an hour or so later. It was at night. I was in pain. Dr. Chester was a tall, fat black man with a bald head and a Chester A. Arthur beard configuration. It looked like the mustache went under his nose, down his cheeks, and grew wider as it climbed up his fat face and tucked itself behind each ear.

Dr. Chester was the first black man I remember talking to. He was also the first black person I encountered in any way whose personality was different from the black people I had seen on television (or from my grandmother's housekeeper, Mitt, the only other black person I knew). So his presence alone was noteworthy. I was naked and nervous and ten. I remember thinking that Dr. Chester was a whole person. He had his facial hair figured out. He was fat. He had a big personality. My parents had none of that. This guy was put together.

Chester was a nice enough guy but now I was standing in the bathroom of my new home in a new town and a large black man had me bent over the counter and was sticking his finger in my ass while my dad watched. I was crying. If you were a stranger and walked in on this scene you would have called the police immediately. If a cop were to barge into this scene, I'm sure my dad would have said, "It's okay. That's my son. We're doctors." And, oh yes, where was my mother during all this? Probably sucking one of a dozen daily cyclamated diet sodas through a straw, doing macramé, or lying on a bed trying to zip her pants up with a pair of pliers. I went to the hospital the next day and Dr. Chester removed my appendix, incorrectly. I have a horizontal scar as opposed to a diagonal one. I think it's out. Who knows? Years later Dr. Chester got into trouble for doing dubious procedures. The whole episode was confusing and inappropriate and probably helped set the template for my relationship with the medical profession in general. My interactions with doctors have always been a little deeper emotionally than the situation calls for.

I moved back east after my second divorce, so when it was time for my yearly exam, I went to see Dr. Metzger.

Metzger was then seventy-five years old. He was semi-retired, teaching medicine and resting on his laurels, whatever they were. He looked like a well-worn piece of Semitic furniture. A little Jewish Buddha. I walked into his office and said, "How you doing, Dr. Metzger?"

"I'm seventy-five!" he said. "How do I look?"

That's who he was. The guy who says that.

"You look good," I said.

"I'm painting now. This is one of mine."

He led me over to an absolutely horrible beach landscape. It was one of many horrible paintings in his office, all of which he obviously had done.

"Nice," I said.

"I love it. It relaxes me," he said, admiring his own work. "How are you, Marc?"

"Not great. My wife left me. . . ."

I sat there and told Dr. Metzger the whole long, sad story of my life at that moment. He listened with his hands crossed in front of him, nodded, looked concerned when my tone called for it, smiled supportively when he felt an opening to do so. When after about fifteen minutes I had outlined the general situation of my mental and emotional life, he looked at me, uncrossed his hands, opened them with a shrug, and said, "People make a mess."

He then started talking about garbage and how much garbage we each generate. I think he may have been paraphrasing a Philip Roth novel, I'm not sure. It was clear that he was one of those parable-dispensing old Jewish men. *People make a mess.* It was clearly meant to be comforting in that detached, charming way narcissistic old Jewish men have. It wasn't, but I felt like he listened as well as a semi-retired old Jewish doctor/amateur painter resting on his laurels could.

Then he examined me. It was quick, stealthy, detached. He had been sticking his rubber-glove-covered finger in asses for fifty years. He probably taught diagnostic finger-banging in a class, the Metzger method: No talking. If it's smooth, keep it to yourself till you're washing up and can explain it.

Everything was fine. I was healthy. Metzger smiled, patted me on the back, and said, "At least you have your health."

I thanked him. As I walked out of his office I thought of it as a mantra almost: "People make a mess. At least I have my health." I repeated it a couple of times in my head. It actually helped. Just as I got out of his office into the reception area I heard Metzger call after me.

"Marc, come back in here."

I walked back into the room.

People make a mess. At least I have my health.

"Sit down for a minute," he said, directing me back to the chair directly in front of his desk.

"Is there a problem, Dr. Metzger?"

"No. There is no problem." He leaned a bit over his desk, pulled his glasses down a bit so his eyes were peering over the top of the frame, and said, "Have you tried Viagra?"

When you're a man this is a loaded question. It implies something about your masculinity. At least in my mind it did.

"I don't need Viagra," I said.

Metzger's face lit up. His being became illuminated. He smiled, grinned actually.

"It's not about need! This is a great drug. It's fun. There are no side effects. Let me give you some."

Metzger explained that he used it and had become born-again hard. I had to picture that for a moment, sadly. A half-empty sack of flour with a protruding hungry nub. He kept extolling the virtues of Viagra, but I'm a drug guy so I didn't need much pushing.

"Okay, give me a few."

I thanked Metzger and left the office again.

People make a mess. At least I have my health and a handful of Viagra.

I knew what Viagra was supposed to do but I had never taken it. When I got home I did some research. It amazed me how much money that drug made for Pfizer, like billions. What that meant to me was that everyone was taking it or at least had tried it. It wasn't just those people you saw on commercials dancing in their living room, holding hands in bathtubs on mountains, or getting onto motorcycles with too much gear. No, the numbers implied that everyone was doing it. So why not me?

I'm not sure there is such a thing as erectile dysfunction. It seems concocted as a means to an end to sell the stuff. Everyone has their ups and downs. Viagra is about an erectile guarantee. That's what you are paying for. In the emotional state that I was in it was perfect. I couldn't understand why they weren't marketing the drug to people in my situation. I pictured the ad campaign.

Viagra, for when you want to fuck anything.
Zoom in. Me sitting at the edge of a bed crying with a hard-on. "I miss my wife. This feels weird. Okay, I'm ready. Sit on it."
Pull out on scantily clad women approaching me.
Viagra, for when you want to fuck anything.

Viagra was amazing. At that point in my life, I'd progressed to being the sort of guy who has to be turned on and deeply attracted to a woman to enjoy sex. I didn't just like to fuck. I liked to fuck souls. I liked to have the kind of sex that is so good that in middle of it you are thinking, "One of us is going to die." That is hard to come by but with Viagra it's right there, always. I didn't have to be sexually attracted to or even like the other person to achieve a triumphant erection—with the drug I just needed to feel a dull spark and before I knew it, I was wrestling with an angry arm in my pants.

The first time I took it I felt estranged from my penis. There were moments when I was having sex on Viagra and I looked down at my dick and thought, "It doesn't even need me." I wished in that moment I could astral-project out of my body and sit on the other side of the room masturbating to me fucking. That's how good I was doing. I was my own porn movie. If you have any sensitivity at all sexually you will see God in the bed when you're using Viagra. After sex on that stuff it's like nodding off on heroin. And that's exactly what I wanted. Why would you ever want to be emotionally engaged, intimate, obsessed, or in love with someone ever again? With Viagra you can shield your heart with your cock and everyone is satisfied.

It was insane. And addictive. In the end, Viagra revealed itself to be the greatest antidepressant created. I realized just how much relationships are built around sexual idiosyncrasies, insecurities, fears, and the coddling of those things between people. Viagra obliterated all that. It is also a lie. One I could live with for a bit. It was saving my life. I was a triumphant fraud with an angry Jew cock out to get some payback. Viagra helped me fuck my wife out of my heart and mind, which I think is a valid therapeutic approach to healing heartbreak.

If you want to fuck away your problems as deeply as possible, here's what I recommend: Order yourself some Indian Viagra. That's right, just answer one of those spam emails and within a week or two you will be sent an exotic parcel in a brown wrapper. You will open it to find a package with some sleazy artwork that looks like something you would get out of a machine in a men's room at a truck stop. This is your medicine. It is cheap, probably bad for you, and effective. Then get out there, tiger.

But it's not all breeze-triggered hard-ons and monster orgasms. There's a dark side to Viagra and it's this: The drug makes your dick a liar. Taking it and not copping to it makes *you* a liar. So you are a lying dick with a lying dick and that has its consequences. The sex is Olympian, but fraudulent. Like porn. After a while, I had to wean myself back to the land of emotion. And that meant that I also had to reassess my relationship with porn.

Porn is a drug, and like any other drug it can ruin your mind and life, especially if you don't realize you're addicted. Sexuality has been unleashed and demystified by things like pornography and Viagra, but I don't think this was Wilhelm Reich's vision of what would happen if repression were destroyed. Sexual freedom has not obliterated neurosis. There are just a whole lot of new neuroses and issues that come from completely untethered sex. Repression might now be the healthier choice—when you deny yourself easy sex, you allow sex to retain its function as a vehicle for intimacy and love as opposed to some kind of athletic pastime with a sure win at the end.

This is coming from a guy who watches porn, occasionally, sometimes compulsively. Just be aware. If you are ever rubbing your hands with excitement and looking forward to your porn time you might be too far gone. I think when you are about to watch porn you should probably be working on something else: your job, a novel, a screenplay, your taxes. When that moment hits you when you say to yourself, "What's the point. This sucks. I suck. It's all bullshit. I'm fucked," then you click over to the porn. When you are falling down the pit of self and the only thing you can do to stop your fall is grab hold of your cock, that's when you should watch porn.

Don't be afraid to let your higher self rise up and out of your body and look down on you and say, "Look at you, sad little man. Locked in a cage of self. Hitting a button for pleasure like a rodent. You should be ashamed of yourself, tragic human." Then let your lower self look up at it, dick in hand, and say, "Fuck you! I'm doing this now. Leave me alone. I'll meet you later and we'll discuss." Just make sure both selves are in attendance to keep your humility in check.

The other thing that worries me about watching porn is that I don't think our brains are built to handle that much fucking. If you sit down and watch porn for a half hour you can see at least fifteen different sexual situations with any number of people involved. How are our brains able to process that? It's complete overload. Picture it like this. You're standing at the end of a hallway. It looks like a hotel hallway. There are fifteen doors along this hallway. All of them are open. You start masturbating at the end of the hallway and start walking. In every room there is some kind of sex going on. You just move from door to door, masturbating. At the end of the hallway you come. If that happened, you would never forget that day for the rest of your life. Now you can do that at home, in front of your computer, in a half hour. That has to be fucking with your head, literally.

I guess what I'm saying is that you don't want to get porn head. This is a psychological condition that is not permanent but happens when you watch too much porn, which detaches your body from your mind, or use drugs like Viagra that detach your mind from your body. The primary symptom is when you find yourself walking into a sexual situation with another human and you have a moment when you think, "Where's the guy?"

Then you catch yourself and realize it's you. You're the guy. This is real life. Feel it.

I'm a Good Person

I have moments where I literally ask myself, "Am I a good person? Really? Am I?"

Then I think, "Well, if I am a good person would I be asking myself that question? Don't good people know that they are good people? If I have time to ruminate, make a list in my head of examples of my bad-personness, then maybe I'm not a good person. I'm not saying that I am a bad person, but why would I question myself?"

People have said: "I know Marc; he means well." He means well? If I'm a good person why would I need this kind of moral interpretation? "Don't mind him; he means well."

But I do mean well.

In my mind I'm running a soup kitchen. I'm building Habitat for Humanity houses wherever they're necessary, even in pestilential war zones. Sometimes I take side trips to Darfur to feed kids. I'm doing a lot of stuff in my head. Maybe I'm at In-N-Out

Burger sitting there stuffing my face. Do I take any actions that would justify me as a good person? Hold on a sec, let me just help this guy in his wheelchair to his table. He's a vet.

"Are you okay, Red? All right, buddy. Well, I'll just be up here at the counter if you need anything. If you want another roll let me know. Let's not yell today. Okay, Captain?"

This is the sort of thing that happens in mind. In my mind, I transcend simple goodness and reach for the beatific. In my mind, I'm very busy with my good works. Not complaining, just busy. But what about real life? How am I measuring up?

I was recently walking down the street in San Francisco and I saw dozens of homeless people. I started to judge them. Who am I going to give money to? Limb missing? You get a dollar. Crackhead or drunk? A quarter. I won't necessarily deny anyone, but I will judge their need based on my own moral compass. I have no consistent policy in place, aside from always giving people with missing limbs money.

I was standing on a subway in New York once when a guy with no legs was rolling his way through the car, low. He was asking for money. The guy standing next to me said, just under his breath, "I'm not giving that guy money. No fucking way." This made me angry. I'm thinking, "What reason could you possibly have for not giving a guy with no legs money?" Is he thinking, *Oh, hell no. I'm not giving that guy money. He's just going to take the money and cut his arms off. I've seen this before. He'll be back next year with no limbs asking for money. I'm not falling for that twice.*

Sometimes I will deny a panhandler based on how many panhandlers I've already run into that day and how many I have given money to. My annoyance factor. As if when I deny someone a donation they know that I might have given someone else money yesterday. It doesn't really matter to that person, but somehow in my head I have justified it.

Do I hold the door open for people? Sure, I do a little of that. Do I say thank you? I try to remember to say thank you. Sometimes I'll go back and say thank you if I've forgotten or skipped out on a favor or act of kindness or service, which I do a lot. It's not that I'm ungrateful, but I kind of am. I'm already on to the next thing. I don't think I have a bad heart, but I'm always wondering what's next, what's next? Me, me, me. Hang on a second.

Stop yelling. I am not the enemy. Now what is it you can't eat again? What are you allergic to? Just peanut butter? All right, there are jelly sandwiches. Take one for later, too, because I know you don't have anywhere to sleep tonight.

There's a lot of good stuff going on in my head.

I don't give blood. Why don't I give blood? I don't know. I should give blood. That's a good thing to do and you get a cookie afterward. Why don't I do some of that?

Just take the hammer that's on the thing. Yeah, the roof looks great. The people are going to be so happy. They are going to be so happy that they have a place to live. I am so proud of all of us for doing this and that God gave us this opportunity.

Why don't I spread some more money around? The Greenpeace people come up to me all the time. They have a real racket going. If you're in a big city, like New York, especially, they hire some of the hottest girls to come up to you on the street.

"Do you care about the whales?"

"Whatever you want, I care about it very much right now. What's your name? I already give to Greenpeace."

I say that even though I stopped giving to them. Does that make me a bad person? Does it? Hold on a minute.

This is your new house. I want to cry, too! Look around; it's yours. Yeah, we built it for you. Yeah. It's yours.

I have got to do better. I have got to get out of my head and get into the world and feed people.

I had a great real-life moment in San Francisco recently. I had gotten up early because I needed to go down to the ferry building where they have the high-end food mall. I wanted to pick up some *guanciale* at Boccalone, some cured pig jowls to make my *all'amatriciana* heart-attack pasta sauce. San Francisco is an odd place for me. With as much time as I have spent there I still don't really have a feel for the streets. There are some dangerous-looking people who lurk around there. On this day, I saw some dude with a hoodie on literally a block away and my radar went off. I thought there was something menacing and troubled and bad about him. He had an energy coming off him that seemed chaotic, angry, needy, and intrusive. I could feel it from a block away.

I had passed the point where I could have casually shuffled across the street without making it seem like I was running away from whatever I thought he was going to do to me. I was locked in. This is the sort of language that was going on in my head:

"You're going to have to face the fire."

As if my life was at stake and there was a good chance in the next minute this guy would stab me and take my money and no one would help me. It would take a long time for the cops to come; a nice man would put his jacket under my head while screaming for someone to call an ambulance.

"Call an ambulance! This man is bleeding!"

It would take the ambulance ten minutes. So I was looking at fifteen to twenty minutes with a knife wound, bleeding on the street, before anything was done. The chances of my survival—depending on where I got cut—were low. All of that was going through my mind while I was walking by this guy. That is what I loaded the cartridge of my head up with.

I looked into his eyes and he looked into mine. Nothing happened.

I think he saw that I knew he was about to stab me and take my money and that I would have trouble getting an ambulance, and he chose not to do it. I'd like to believe that. I also knew from the look in his eyes that he was desperate for something and that he'd been awake for a really long time. It was scary.

Then I realized that he was standing right next to an ATM and there was a woman using the ATM. There weren't that many people on the street. Despite the fact that what I was thinking might have been fantasy I did linger there a little bit just past the ATM and looked back at him to make sure that he knew there was a witness to whatever he was thinking about doing in that moment when that woman was getting her money.

On some level that makes me a good person. When the woman finished, the dangerous man stepped up to the machine and put his card in . . . hold on a second . . .

Hello, kids. Hello, kids. Hi! Who's hungry? Who's hungry? Come on, gather around. It's nice to see you all again. Hello.

I'm helping people.

★ 15 ★

Hummingbirds
and the Killer of Mice

A while back I was going through the stuff that had been left at my house when I bought it. There were two hummingbird feeders in a box of other crap. They were the glass-bottle type with the fake red flowers at the bottom. I decided to clean them up and get them outside. I had nothing better to do. Okay, that's a lie. I had plenty to do. As a self-employed creative type it is remarkable how many activities I will engage in other than being creative and self-employed: cleaning, scouring, organizing, emailing, tweeting, anything. That day it was refurbishing a couple of hummingbird feeders. I was going to feed the fucking hummingbirds. That was the plan. That was the attitude I had. There was spite in my spirit, not against them, but I needed them to appreciate what I was doing. That was the gratification I was looking for.

When I was sitting there putting together these hummingbird feeders I found myself saying, "They better come. I'm doing this for them. I don't even know if they are out there, but these little fast-flying fuckers better come and slurp this shit up that I'm putting out there for them." I had a lot of expectations and felt like some part of my self was on the line. That's how insecure I am. The thought of being rejected by hummingbirds was too much for my sensitive artistic ego to deal with given that I was spending all this time putting together these feeders. All this time being about a half hour.

I did some research. Hummingbird feed is just tap water and sugar, a quarter cup of sugar to a cup of water. You have to use tap water for the minerals. You create the mixture and fill up the feeders. The red liquid stuff they sell at pet stores is just a racket.

So I built the feeders, mixed the feed, filled them up, and put them out. Sure enough, the little fast-flying fuckers came. They are fascinating. I've actually sat and watched hummingbirds for more than an hour. While working—in my mind—on other more creative things, of course.

Once you spend enough time with hummingbirds you start to see they are vicious little bastards. They are nasty little fuckers. I had no idea. They are unique in the way they move in the air, hover, and flit around. Their wings go so fast they seem to be floating and at first you think it's so precious. They are pristine and gorgeous, with that whirring sound *zzzzzzz*. But let me tell you something: They're vicious bastards.

I have feeders hung near the back and the front doors of my home. About a hundred feet down the hill at the back of my house is a large tree. The birds perch in the tree, three or four of them in different parts of it. When they're hungry, they fly from the tree and dive-bomb into the feeders. When one is at the feeder and another comes up they'll start dogfighting. There are hummingbird wars. No one talks about the hummingbird wars. Well, I'm going to talk about it. There is a problem in the hummingbird world. These birds are beating the shit out of each other. They are dogfighting and dive-bombing each other. It's like watching a very small and adorable version of *Top Gun*.

They aren't really threatened by people, either. A hummingbird stood me down. I walked out into my backyard and he was whizzing and stopping at the feeder. I walked right up to him and he hovered in front of me at eye level, stared right into my face like *Do you have a problem? Maybe you should go.* I had to step back. I didn't know if he was going to poke my eyes out and suck out my ocular jelly. Who the hell knew with these animals? Vicious little bastards.

It kind of makes me respect them. They have a veneer that says "Look at me how precious and cute and small I am. I'm just a perfect little being," while underneath they are really "Get the fuck out of the way, I'm doing this." We developed an understanding: I was their customer. I got to watch them from time to time, but I had to pay up with feed or they'd pluck me blind.

Long after I put the feeders out and the birds and I had settled into our territories and respective roles, I was sitting at my dining room table plinking away on the keys, doing the business. I was probably justifying to myself that social networking is work, even three hours of social networking. And that's when I heard that sound, the resonating percussive *donk* of a bird hitting the window.

I knew it would happen eventually with those birds out front all the time dive-bombing and dogfighting. When I went out to look, sure enough, sitting on the ground on the front patio was a hummingbird. I knew he was hurt but he was just sitting on the ground looking around. It didn't look like his neck was broken, but he was just sitting there. When you see a bird just sitting there, not flying, not walking, you think: That bird's fucked. It's going to die. What do I do?

My first thought was to put him in a shoe box and bring him to the vet like when I found a dead bird when I was seven, but I would have to have my mom drive me and she lives in Florida. That never panned out even then. It was just my parents' way of teaching me about death before I knew any humans who died.

I knew not to touch it. I had heard if you touch a bird they're screwed because apparently they are rejected by the rest of the bird community and then they die alienated in some sort of bird shame Siberia. These hummingbirds seem like violent loners anyway, but I was still worried. What if I touched it and it did fly away—would it ever be able to get laid again? I was so confused. I stopped myself from looking for some kind of hummingbird hotline to call for help. I didn't want to get involved with the bird equivalent of cat ladies.

Sadly, my next thought was to let my cat LaFonda out and give this bird the ending it deserved. It seemed logical. I'm not abdicating my responsibility to this little creature; I'm just working as nature's middleman here. I'm going to let LaFonda go out there and take care of this bird. If I were an animal I would want that, to go out like animals go out, fighting for my life.

But this bird was handicapped and what does that make me? A heartless bastard. Let's just let the predator, LaFonda, the vicious little bitch that she is, go out there and start ripping this thing to shreds. She would probably keep it alive to play with it for two hours, prolonging its suffering as long as possible. Something inside of me said that's not right.

I have a hard time with dying animals. I get attached to animals. But after a certain point you have to be able to let them go and do the right thing. People who grew up on farms know this.

Years ago I worked in a coffee shop in Harvard Square called the Coffee Connection. It was a pre-Starbucks fancy coffee shop. They were very snobby about their coffee selection there, beans from all over the world. They only served you coffee if you sat down in the restaurant. They'd serve them in French presses and every coffee had special instructions for brewing. It was all very high-end and annoying.

Of course, I worked there with a bunch of artists, or, more accurately, people who spent all their time not doing their art. This wasn't yet the time of the hipsters; these were just your regular college town young people working in a coffee shop—a lot of big dreams, a lot of big talk, a lot of philosophies and ideas. A lot of people who were pretending that they knew about life but I could tell they didn't. At least I'd been to Los Angeles, so I already had one experience of being chewed up and spat out by life.

I had a chip on my shoulder. I was that guy. I was the barista who was already bitter at twenty-two. *I used to live in Los Angeles. I used to hang out with Kinison.* Now I was the guy angrily frothing milk, pulling espresso, and washing dishes. I used to open the place and I remember one morning getting there a little late and the whole staff was behind the counter. There was the gay guy— I'm not defining him by his sexuality, but he was demonstrably effeminate. There was Peter, and his girlfriend. Peter was a painter and she was a painter's girlfriend. There was the odd chef with too much hair who always wore sunglasses. I remember they were all standing in a circle behind the counter when I walked in and asked them what was going on.

They were all huddled together looking at a mouse stuck on a sticky trap. It was splayed out, immobilized and twitching. They were all standing around looking at it saying, "It's so sad. What do we do? What do we do?"

I don't know where this came from or what happened to me but I just stepped in and stomped on the mouse with my foot. I smashed it. Then I picked it up and threw it away.

All of them were like "What the fuck? Why would you . . . ?"

That's what needed to be done. And they never looked at me the same. I was like Colonel Kurtz of the Coffee Connection. I had done something willful and morally dubious. I had made an example. I had transgressed. I was the killer of mice. But killing that mouse was ultimately an ethical solution. What are the options at that point? Throw it in the garbage and prolong its suffering? I try to find ethical solutions to dealing with the tiny little lives infesting our own, but it's not always possible. I remember having a conversation with my buddy Jim back in the day. He grew up in Montana or somewhere. At the time, I had this mouse problem in my Queens apartment and wasn't sure what to do about it. Jim said, "What's wrong with you? They're vermin. They're like bugs. You kill them."

I said, "No, they're not. They're rodents. They are more fun than bugs. Much more expressive. Bugs are disgusting."

Jim was right, but not for the reason he thought he was. I had slowly come to realize that I had to kill this mouse because it fucked with me and insulted my intelligence. That's where I draw a line with these things.

The mouse seemed to be hanging out in this one bowl that had a rag in it. It looked like it was sleeping in there when I was asleep, like the bowl was its own little bed, the rag its blanket. Sure, it would shit around the house a bit, but fuck it. I used to like seeing it scurry across the floor. It was my friend. I didn't name him, but he was hanging out. I felt like I could live with it. We were cohabitating. There was no reason I had to kill the mouse.

Then one morning, I woke up. I went to the fridge, to the freezer to get the coffee out, and saw mouse shit on top of the refrigerator. *How the fuck did a mouse shit on top of the refrigerator?* I swear to God, folks, I sat there and I could not figure out how that mouse had gotten to the top of the refrigerator to shit. It was almost like he was shitting at me. Like, we're friends but I'm going to push the envelope a little bit.

I didn't know if he flew there or if there was a series of some sort of Rube Goldberg devices that he used to get on top. Maybe there was a bunch of mice and they were flipping each other up. I don't know. All I know is that I didn't know and I took it as a line drawn in the sand. You have baffled me; I can't understand how you did this. It's disgusting and it's obviously antagonistic and I'm going to fucking kill you.

So I put a sticky trap out and I got him and I suffocated him. I didn't let him suffer too much.

I felt awful.

I wouldn't call myself an animal lover. I can anthropomorphize almost anything, sometimes inanimate objects. But when I build a relationship with a certain animal, of any kind, I grow to respect it. All I ask is for them to show up for their side of the relationship.

After I decided not to unleash the fury of my demented cat onto the crippled hummingbird, I went out to see how badly it was hurt. I walked out the front door and looked at the bird and it looked at me. And then it took off. *Zzzzzzzzzz boom*, gone. It had been sitting down there for like five minutes. What the hell was that about? Why didn't it just fly away in the first place? Was it stunned?

Then I thought it was probably feeling ashamed of itself. It hit the window. It was probably just sitting on the porch thinking, "I'm an idiot. I can't fucking believe I hit the window. I hope Goose and Maverick didn't see that. I'm just going to lie low, let this blow over, maybe they won't bust my balls later at base. I don't want to be that guy, the guy that hit the window. It's bad enough we have to fight for the stupid fake flowers and the sugar water, and I have to be the guy that hit the window? I'm just going to hang out and lie low—whoa, it's the supplier guy? I'm out of here."

He flew away humbled. And I think that's the message here. That's an animal fable about humility. If you survive your mistake, you must learn from it. Accept that you're fragile, vulnerable, and sometimes stupid. Realize that you're not immortal and you've got to take care of yourself. And then laugh it off and fly away.

★ 16 ★

Dunk the Clown

Recently I went to the Levi's store in San Francisco, which I believe is the original Levi's store. The source. There is something about the Levi's label that is imprinted deeply in my mind and heart. I don't buy Levi's that often but when I was a kid it seemed like they were the only pants. You had your Lees, your Wranglers, and then the Calvin Klein invasion, but Levi's represented something with integrity, something American, but American in the best way possible. Something of value that lasted. Now everything turns to garbage inside a couple of years. Planned obsolescence has forever denied us the ability to believe in workmanship, institutions, and lifetime guarantees. This is true with everything from pants to marriages. And obviously life itself.

When I was a kid and my mom bought me Levi's they were stiff and uncomfortable for weeks. Then over time and multiple washings, they'd fade the way you wanted them to and start to contour themselves to your body. They became more than your pants.

They were your skin. They grew with you. They saw what you saw, absorbed your pain, mistakes, spills, and slides. They scarred and ripped with you. It seemed like they lasted forever. Some part of me can't understand why I ever got rid of that pair of Levi's that I had in seventh grade. How did I lose track of those pants? I would wear Levi's until they were just tatters. I don't know if I am romanticizing, mythologizing, or being nostalgic. I assume all three. That seems to be how the brain breaks things down after a certain age.

I went to the Levi's store because I had heard that good jeans were back. That they were making them like they used to. They cost a lot more but if you want some emotional time travel and believe that denim in its raw form can make you feel whole, it's going to cost you to buy that two-legged vessel to a simpler time.

So at the Levi's store I wanted to try on these new stiff jeans. The clerk helping me was a chubby fellow with a handlebar mustache. I have no patience for contemporary handlebar mustaches. They anger me. They look indulgent and ridiculous. Anytime I see one all I can imagine is the guy twisting away at the waxed curls in his mirror like a villain of self-avoidance. If you have a handlebar mustache, that is pretty much all you are. You are a delivery system for a handlebar mustache. I saw a guy in Brooklyn once with a handlebar mustache, pierced ears, a fedora hat, and jodhpurs. He was a collage of sartorial attempts at evading himself. It looked like he was interrupted during a shave in the mid-1850s and had to grab some clothes and dress quickly, while being chased through a time tunnel.

The mustache asked me what I was looking for and I told him I had heard that Levi's was making real jeans again. Like the kind I grew up wearing. He said they were but they had to be treated a very specific way. He then told me he was wearing them. I looked down and he was packed pretty snugly into his pants. It made me uncomfortable for a lot of reasons, but I wanted to hear him out.

He told me that his jeans, made with new shrink-to-fit denim, had never touched water.

"You never wash your pants?"

"Nope. I'm going on a year."

I thought, "What does that even mean? You never wash your pants? Don't your pants smell like balls? You probably smell like a ball factory! Do you have immaculate balls? Balls stink if you give them time and now you're wearing your pants for a year? Do you have friends? Does anyone want to hang out with you?" I thought the *mustache* was alienating. I stepped back from him. I didn't catch a wave of bad-ball smell coming off him, but how could it not be there, waiting, a miasma circling his body, if he doesn't want to wash his pants?

I held up the pair of stiff jeans and said, "Well, what do I do with these?" The mustache got very serious.

"What I usually do is I buy them a size smaller than I wear."

This is ridiculous because they are supposed to shrink to fit so you are supposed to buy a size bigger. I can tell I'm not going to wear my pants like his. So he says, "You put the pants on and you get into a bathtub with them. Then you get out of the bathtub and you towel off and then you wear them around, wet, for as long as it takes them to dry. That way they are contoured perfectly to your body. After that you don't wash them, ever. If they get skanky you throw them in the freezer."

I thought the whole pitch was ridiculous but of course I was secretly obsessed with the idea of perfect pants. I am secretly obsessed with the idea of perfect anything to the point that I am always a little disappointed and I think that everyone else has the perfect thing even though clearly the mustache did not have perfect pants because they smelled like balls. I assumed. The entire undertaking sounded ridiculous but I am weak and searching

and desperate, just once, to have a perfect thing. So I bought the
pants.

I'd tried before to find perfection and had my heart broken. I love
my Red Wing boots. I bought a pair of Gentleman Travelers in
oxblood color and wore the hell out of them and then bought
another pair of the exact same shoes. I had a glorious moment
when I bought those boots, standing in the shoe store thinking,
with complete sincerity and faith, *Holy shit my life is going to be
okay with these boots. Everything makes sense.*

There is an ideology that comes with Red Wing boots. I get to
bring them to the Red Wing store whenever I want. They will
polish them. They will oil them up. They will fix whatever needs
to be fixed. If it's a manufacturing problem they will fix them for
nothing. I'm going to have a lifetime relationship with my Red
Wing guy. I built an entire belief system around these fucking
boots.

I was a few weeks into this new pair before I admitted to myself
that there was something wrong. I didn't think they were the right
size. I was walking around and they felt a little big. I should have
bought them a little tighter.

I'd invested in the company, in the boot. I'd invested money
and now I felt my feet just moving around in the boots. They were
not hurting. They were not rubbing on anything. They were fine,
really. But because everything in my life at that moment was
chaos and I was exhausted, my brain saw it as a fine opportunity
for obsession. My brain loves obsessions. If it can make me hate
myself, then it's all the better. So now I had these boots on my feet
that basically as I walked were saying, "You're an idiot. You are an
idiot. It's not our fault, we're a good boot! You didn't think it
through. We're not for your foot. You're not a Red Wing man, or
a man at all for that matter. Now we're being dragged along by

you and your bad disposition because you didn't think it through. You're making us look bad." I had little haters on my feet. I know they are good boots and I know it's not their fault. All I was doing is thinking about my fucking feet and whether or not the boots fit right. I became completely consumed with it.

In the end, I had to admit defeat. The boots went on a shelf. Nothing made sense.

This time, it would be different. The day I got home from San Francisco with my new Levi's, I went online to do a little research. What if the guy was right? Sure enough the consensus on the Internet was that to make these jeans perfect, you put them on, get into a bathtub full of water, and then let them dry while you wear them around. I ran the water into the tub. I don't ever take baths. I can't remember the last time I did and now here I was, taking one with my pants on.

As I was lying in the tub with my new gray Levi's shrink-to-fit pants on, my natural feelings of desperation and stupidity were mixed with another emotion: hope. My life had narrowed in this moment to one small, attainable purpose, the pursuit of perfect jeans, and I felt excited. I also felt empty. This is what my life has become? Don't I have better things to do? I am a forty-eight-year-old man in a bathtub wearing pants thinking I will be a better person for owning a pair of highly personalized jeans. It was in that moment that it hit me. These pants are just pants. They aren't going to do anything special.

That guy with the fancy mustache at the Levi's store was a carnival barker at the Dunk the Clown game. The clown was the me who bought the pants and the bullshit that came with them. The pitcher with the ball whom I was taunting was the me who knew better. I took the pants off and enjoyed the bath. In the tank, again.

17

I Want to Understand Opera

I want to understand opera. I don't like all of this disposable entertainment, Twitter feeds and TV shows and Angry Birds. I want to see stuff that has been entertaining people for centuries, that offers its audience meaning that allows them to rise above the rabble; art that elevates the human spirit. But opera is almost always in another language and, to me, that is a fatal deterrent. How much can I enjoy it if I don't understand what they're saying? That's a nice song, I think, those are good costumes, that guy seems to be upset about something.

Maybe opera is not the thing I'm looking for.

How about ballet? That's cultural. Why don't I go see some ballet? Because I don't really understand ballet beyond the point where she's spinning around and, oh, she's flying and the guy caught her. He didn't drop her! That has to be half the appeal of ballet—watching people fly into each other's arms and not get dropped. Or secretly hoping they do drop. That's not art, it's more like athletics, which I don't get beyond grudging admiration of extreme physical accomplishments. Modern dance is interesting if it's not silly.

Perhaps I should see more theater but there's nothing worse than bad theater. Have you ever had to sit through a bad play? Bad theater is torture by another name. If the acting is bad I feel sorry for the actors. If the play is poorly written I feel embarrassed for everyone involved, including the audience, and wonder why someone doesn't get onstage and help them. Like when a boxing trainer throws in the towel when his fighter is getting badly beaten. I have been at a play and thought, "Someone should put a stop to this." Have you ever had that feeling when you're watching a play? *I'm going up there, enough is enough.* Sadly, if you are at a bad play it is usually because someone you know has brought you. Or worse, you have a friend in the show. That's always a tricky chat backstage afterward; being the person who'd actually stopped the play midway through would probably make it even more awkward.

The point is, maybe I need to re-immerse myself in fine arts. They're magic. It doesn't always work but the good stuff, or at least the stuff that resonates, should engage your heart in a way that can reflect, sate, define, amplify, provoke, or relieve what seems like chaos or confusion in your life. The art allows you to experience it and better understand your own undefined or renegade emotions. Sometimes the art gives you new things to worry about. That's some good art there.

Then again, maybe I have enough drama in my life.

I recently almost broke up with my girlfriend, Jessica. Here's something I learned about myself. I don't know how to break up with people. It's new to me; I don't know how to do it and to be quite honest with you, if I'm left to my own devices I will never break up with anyone. I will marry a person I'm sure I shouldn't be marrying before I'll break up with them, which is unfair to everybody involved.

Here's the problem: If somebody likes me a lot, why wouldn't I want to have them around, even if I don't like them as much? It's very nice to be liked.

Every day you say, "Hey, how's it going?"

"I like you."

"Cool, thanks for hanging out."

Unfortunately, if that goes on too long it becomes, "Hey, what's going on?"

"I like you."

"Why? I'm nothing but a dick to you because I don't like you as much. Why do you still like me?"

"I like you even more now and will desperately cling to you forever."

Then you are really screwed. Then you have to figure out how to blow up the situation or try to be an adult. And of course you want to be an adult, but how do you break up without drama? That's the big question. And there is no answer. So instead I just create as much drama as possible, as much chaos, as much pain as I can, until the point arrives when the person says, "I can't put up with this shit anymore. I'm leaving."

Of course, that is the moment when I realize I can't live without them.

Wait, you're saying, there *is* an adult way to break up. Why wouldn't you just say, "Look, I just don't think this is working out and I think we've been through a lot together and it's been fun, but I just don't think there's a future in it and I'm sorry"? Ah, but that's when they start crying and I say, "Oh, don't cry. Why are you upset? Okay, let's just keep going. I'm an asshole."

That's the problem. I would rather just push it to the limit and then push it some more till it all blows up. That's my opera. That's my theater.

So this is what happened. I had been fighting with Jessica for about twenty minutes. I have no idea what it was about. Does it even matter at that point? You're just gunning for make-up sex after the fifteen-minute mark. This is the scene.

I was standing by the door of my house on the inside. The door was open and the screen was closed. The windows of the house were open. Jessica was standing inside the house saying, "Stop talking."

I said, "Get the fuck out of my house."

"Just stop fucking talking."

"Get out of my house. Now."

"I don't have to get out of your house."

That baffled me. In my moment of confusion I noticed someone walking up the driveway, a Latino man. He had his arms raised up over his head as he walked up on my front porch. He looked upset. I stepped out the door. I said, "What's up, man?"

He pleaded almost desperately, "Please stop fighting. They are going to call the police up the street."

"They don't need to do that. We're cool. Just an argument here."

It was then I realized his arms were raised to indicate he was an unarmed civilian. He didn't want to get involved in what was potentially a violent situation from his point of view. He thought he was being brave and wanted to make sure I knew he came in peace. I was slightly offended. I am not a physical abuser. Emotional abuse is my thing. I have my principles.

Then the stranger started crying.

"What's up, man?" I said, looking back into the house at Jessica, who was keeping her distance, looking confused but still trying to hold on to the anger and spirit of the argument.

"I just lost my wife," he cried.

What does he mean "lost," I wondered. Did she die or did she leave him? I would temper my sympathy appropriately. But in the end it didn't matter. There was a crying man on my porch.

"I'm sorry to hear that. I really am."

The man pulled himself together a bit and then cried out to me, "Do you love her?"

I thought, "This is an awkward way for her to hear it the first time," but the situation demanded it.

I called back into the house. "I love you, baby. The guy is crying here."

"Just be kind, please," he said.

I got it. He was some kind of weird angel.

"Okay, man. I will. Thanks."

"Okay, I'm sorry."

"No problem. Tell the neighbors not to call the police, please."

"Yes, yes I will," he said as he walked off my porch and down the driveway. Arms down.

I walked back into the house. Jessica shrugged. "What just happened?"

I just looked at her, stunned and ashamed. The arc of the fight had been interrupted. The natural, mutual abuse cycle had been hijacked by a stranger's emotions. There were no tears; no one had to leave. There was no lost love to be earned back. There was just an awkward silence hanging between us. Something had to be said. It was a potentially profound moment that we could grow from. We sat down across from each other. Minutes passed.

"I wish they'd call the police," Jessica said. Still angry.

"Why?"

"So you'd stop talking."

I let it sink in. I wasn't going to pick up where we left off. It was on me to say something that would bring us closer. I watched this come out of my mouth.

"You know, if we are going to do this we really need to close the windows."

That was my epiphany. She smiled.

"Definitely," she said.

That's why we are together. It's clearly love. Now whenever I get that metallic pre-rage tone in my voice, Jessica jumps up from whatever she is doing and runs around the house saying, "Close the windows!" It works. We fight less. How can I be mad when she is so adorable, hopping onto her toes to push down all the windows? It disarms me completely.

If that scene were depicted in a play I think I would hug the stranger on the porch and hold him before he walks away. If it were an opera I believe he would have wings and be lowered into the scene on a wire. If it were it a musical I would think all the neighbors would come out of their houses at the end and surround my porch. Jessica and I would come out of the front door holding hands and singing:

Her: We'll close the windows! He'll stop talking.

Me: I will stop talking.

Together: We're sorry. We're crazy. It's human. Who are you to judge?

Neighbors: They're right. It's human.

Everyone: We're human. It happens.

Curtain.

18

I Almost Died #1: Cleveland

I almost died on a plane recently. At least I think I almost died. In my mind I almost died and that's all that's important.

I used to be afraid to fly but at some point I realized that I just don't have the energy for it anymore. I have better things to do with my brain. So I stopped worrying and when the planes still took off and flew and landed, even without my emotionally and mentally flying them from my seat, I realized that maybe I hadn't really been in charge all along. This was one of the most powerful spiritual revelations I have had in my life. The moment that I knew in my soul that nothing I was doing in my head had any bearing on actual events or possible outcomes, I was suddenly free. I was no longer seized with visions of wings catching fire, wings falling off, planes in tailspins, planes falling out of the sky, planes blowing up or colliding in midair. I was no longer gaming out these disasters in my mind, finding ways to miraculously survive and, depending on the situation, perhaps saving many people in the process. The fact that I don't obsessively ruminate on these scenarios anymore is an indication I have grown spiritually. I have no control over the plane or anything else really. I am okay with that. Every bump is not the beginning of the end. I move through it. I deal.

On the day I almost died I had to take an afternoon flight to Cleveland. I don't like flying in the afternoon because the probability of delay is high. If it's an afternoon flight, I know that "weather" in Denmark means I'm going to be delayed out of LAX for some reason. I don't know if there are too many planes in the air at all times or if we're going through extreme weather because of climate change or if the pilots have all just become frightened. I seem to remember a time when planes would fly through anything. I swear I have childhood memories of landing in snowdrifts and flying through thunderstorms. I have a vague recollection of taking off in fire. Just fire on both sides of the plane. I was screaming and my mom was saying, "We're up. We're up. It's okay." I also watched a lot of Vietnam War coverage as a little kid so I may have things confused in my mind.

Before I left my house for the airport I checked the weather in Cleveland so I could mentally prepare for the likelihood of sitting around the airport. There was a storm moving into Cleveland. I was doomed to pay for Wi-Fi at LAX.

But surprisingly, we took off on time. Once we were in the air the pilot got on the mic and said, "Welcome aboard. We may hit some weather getting into Cleveland but I think we are going to just miss it." He had a cockiness to his voice. It sounded like he was excited about the possible challenge. I thought, "Then why are you telling us? Are we supposed to sit here for hours wondering how this story ends?"

There was no Wi-Fi on the plane, which I found aggravating because that meant I had to read and write and think as opposed to tweet and email and IM. Kicking it old-school is a drag on my need for immediate gratification but I settled in. They had DirecTV so I was safe from actually getting anything done.

It was dark out. Our plane was about an hour outside Cleveland when the pilot got back on the mic and said, "Could the flight attendants please prepare the cabin for landing and take their seats. Looks like we are going to hit that weather." So he didn't make it. Then the flight attendants told all of us to fasten our seat belts. I was watching the movie *Woodstock* on VH1. I was blasting it into my head as loud as it would go. Joe Cocker was singing "With a Little Help from My Friends" when I saw lightning on both sides of the plane. At first I thought it was the blinking lights on the wings, but no. It was lightning. Lightning is not good for planes.

I didn't freak out. I knew we might be in for something but was consoled by my new understanding of things: I had no control over what happened. Plus, I had been through turbulence before; it's survivable. Then, as Cocker reached the song's crescendo, screaming, "I get high with a little help from my friends, / I get by with a little help from my friends," the plane lunged downward for a good five seconds.

Now I was out of my head, out of Woodstock, back in the present, gripping my armrests. Nothing gets you in the present like terror. There was another layer of sound entering my head from outside the headset. It was the man behind me screaming, "Oh, no! Oh, God, no!" His shouts were percussive and each outburst came just after a bump or tilt of the plane, which now seemed to be completely out of control.

I did not scream, not yet. I had a series of odd thoughts as adrenaline blasted through my body. "Do I want to die to this song? It's a good song but do I want to die to it? What song would be a good song to die to? I should make a death playlist for my iPod for when I have time to decide before I die what song I want to hear. I'm an older guy. I could be on a treadmill and feel a pain shooting down my arm. *Better pick a tune, fast.*" Then I thought, "My girlfriend. I wish she was here. This is something we should be doing together. Dying." I didn't want her to miss the terror I was going through. That is a metaphor for every adult relationship I've had. "Hey baby, we're going down. Get in."

You don't choose your scream. No one practices it. It is involuntary and spontaneous. You don't know what will come out of you and you can only hope for the best. The guy behind me had set a pretty low bar. He was whimpering with sporadic outbursts of high-pitched screaming followed by apologies. I didn't want to be that guy. So when the plane dropped out of the sky again and fell for a few seconds, I am happy to report that what came out of me, at the moment when I was terrified to my core, was a brash, loud "Oh, come on!" I can live with that. I didn't gloat. I didn't turn to the guy behind me and say, "That's how a man screams. You should put a lid on that little girl inside of you and get hold of yourself." I just stayed seized in my seat hoping to get through it. When the storm started tossing the plane around back and forth I did let out a couple of other grunting yelps. I did scream out an "Are you fucking kidding me!" followed by a "Jesus, not like this!" Which is odd because he's not even my guy. My people come from the father. The original. But "Jesus" is so catchy. I think I would have gotten some odd looks if I yelled, "Yahweh, no!"

The pilot finally got under the clouds. He made it through the storm. Cleveland was in view. He started to circle the city. I could feel him flying, back in control. It felt like he was having fun. The plane was fairly empty. I was in my own row and the woman across from me was in her own row. The guy behind me was alone as well. As the pilot soared and swung the craft around the city I was relieved.

I hated that pilot, though. In my mind he had gambled with

our lives. In my mind the tower had told him to divert to another city and he said, "Fuck that. I got this." Then he turned his radio off.

I turned to the woman and said, "He's taking a victory lap." She smiled awkwardly. Then I made the mistake of asking, "Was everyone screaming up there?" I had my headphones on and couldn't really hear anyone but the guy behind me.

She said, "No. Just you two."

That was a sad moment. Now I had to bond with the guy. We had lived through something. Maybe no one felt the urgency that we did. Maybe they were all numb or in denial, dead inside. Our culture does that to people. I turned around in my seat and said, "You okay, man?" He said, "Yeah, I just can't handle that shit." I said, "Yeah, that was as bad as I have ever been through."

He said, "I'm sorry."

"No worries," I said.

He was a balding middle-aged guy with a beard and a tie-dyed shirt on. Looked like the type of guy who made his own ice cream and cried when Jerry Garcia died. This long strange trip that we were on was not a good one.

When the plane finally landed I was shaken up and aggravated and still trying to come down myself; I had not yet landed. I was still in the air and frightened. I kind of wanted the pilot to validate my experience when he got on the mic. I'm not sure what I wanted him to say. "Wow, that was some bullshit, people. We were freaking out up here, too. You guys all good? My copilot shit his pants and is still crying. I don't think I can go on flying. Sorry." I didn't get anything like that. What I got was "Welcome to Cleveland. Local time is twelve-oh-six." I thought, "Fuck you! You're not taking that experience away from me. Own it!"

Once we were on the ground the head flight attendant made her way through the cabin asking if everyone was okay. I said, "That was pretty bad, no?"

"The worst I've ever been through," she said.

"How long have you been doing this?" I asked.

"Thirty years."

"Holy shit!" I thought. It *was* as bad as it felt. We did almost die.

The woman across the aisle had pulled up a Doppler map on her iPhone and said, "Look at this." I took the phone. There was a storm crescent descending on Cleveland. A big red band of bad with a small break in it, a sliver on the screen. That's when I realized that our pilot was up there, saw that gap, and said, "Fuck it. We can do this!" I was right! He was a hotdogger.

When we pulled into the gate I knew I had to say something. I was in the back of the plane so I was going to be one of the last to walk out. I didn't know what I was going to say but I wanted to share my discomfort and angry gratitude for what I had been through. I felt my thoughts congealing into a fist.

When I got up to the open cockpit door and looked in at the pilot and the copilot packing up their special pilot briefcases, this is what came out of my mouth:

"You guys have fun up there?"

It came out a little too angry to be funny. I sounded like an old man reprimanding children. *You have fun up there with your midair shenanigans?* The pilot looked at me squarely, smiled, and said, "Yes, we did!" His came out a little too angry, too.

I really didn't like him. He was mocking my feelings.

I got my bag and went out to the curb to wait for my car. I saw the screaming man from the plane waiting for a bus. We had a moment. He was clearly still ashamed but relieved, as was I. We looked at each other like we shared a secret hell. *Nam, man. Never forget.* It was as if he was looking at me with that mixture of pleading and trust that this would remain between us with a hint of "take care of yourself, man."

When I got to the hotel it was 12:30 A.M. The storm that we had flown through was just now hitting the city. It was bad: sideways rain, thunder and lightning. I couldn't sleep. I was jacked. I had almost died. I felt like crying. I was thinking almost-just-died thoughts: I have to be nicer to people, I should be grateful, my life is pretty good, I have a sweet girlfriend, I live in the freest country in the world if you can afford it.

I didn't know what to do with all that aggravated/elated life energy. I decided to masturbate.

Ninety-nine percent of the time when you masturbate in a hotel alone it is a sad thing. Not that time. That was the 1 percent. It was a celebration. *Of life*. I didn't watch porn. I didn't even think about fucking. I jerked off to being alive! I think in the middle of it I grunted, "I'm alive. Goddamnit, I'm alive."

I want to be honest, even at the risk of alienating some of you. I came right on the floor of my hotel room.

When I finished I called my girlfriend. I told her what had happened. She was upset. She was almost crying. "Are you okay?" she asked.

"Yeah, I just jerked off."

"That's good, right?" she asked.

"Yeah, I feel better."

"Good."

"Um, I came on the floor of my hotel room."

"Why did you cum on the floor?" she asked, concerned.

"Because that's what freedom feels like sometimes. I'm alive."

19

I Almost Died #2:
"Mouth Cancer"

Don't google "mouth cancer images." Just don't do it. I did. It was bad.

I was in a hotel room in Madison, Wisconsin. This is not important. I am in a lot of hotel rooms. But there I was, in a hotel room in Madison, Wisconsin, just sitting there trying to get some work done and looking forward to my lobby waffle. Those of you who travel and stay at a certain kind of hotel understand the beauty of the lobby waffle. When you're checking in and eyeball a waffle maker in the free-breakfast-buffet nook, some part of you thinks, "How bad could tomorrow be?" I know that at 9:58 the next morning, two minutes before that buffet closes, I will be making my own waffle and it will feel like my birthday for about twenty minutes.

So I'm in the room doing my work. I'm tweeting, updating statuses, emailing, you know, working. Putting in the time to push my slightly damaged, emotionally complicated, inconsistent brand out into the big hungry ether for people to judge and bear witness.

It amazes me that we are all on Twitter and Facebook. By "we" I mean adults. We're adults, right? But emotionally we're a culture of seven-year-olds. Have you ever had that moment when you are updating your status and you realize that every status update is just a variation on a single request: "Would someone please acknowledge me?" You post it and you just wait it out. That first thumbs-up appears. *Like!* Yes. All comments are then read as "We see you, Marc. We love you, Marc. We care that you are there, Marc." Twitter and Facebook are my techno-parents, sating the child in me. But they are not beyond abusing him.

As I worked I was also eating licorice candy compulsively.

I have a short menu of compulsive behaviors now that alcohol and drugs are out of my life, but the key is that something has to be going into my mouth or touching my body every waking second. I can eat compulsively, I can masturbate compulsively, or I can nap compulsively. I know compulsive napping sounds like a contradiction in terms but it is not. I also call them panic naps. A panic nap usually comes on with an exacerbated declaration of:

"Fuck, I gotta . . . goddamnit . . . I can't think about . . . shit, I'm tired."

Licorice was the compulsion of the day. It was fancy licorice, from Italy, almost inedible if you don't have the taste for it but if you do, it's completely addictive. As I sat and ate and tweeted and plinked away on the keys, my tongue was wandering around my mouth sucking on awful candy and I felt a sore spot in my mouth. I thought, "What is that? Did I bite my lip? Is that a canker sore? What is that?" I went to the bathroom, pushed my face toward the mirror, and pulled my lower lip down to see what the problem was. There in my mouth were three red sores surrounded by a brownish ring. It looked nasty. Out loud I said, "Fuck, is that mouth cancer?"

In about eight minutes I went through all five stages of grief, accompanied by panicky grunts. Denial: "That's not mouth cancer. I couldn't have mouth cancer." Anger: "Fuck, I have mouth cancer. What else could it be." Bargaining: "God, I know I don't really believe in you but please let this not be mouth cancer. I will do anything!" Depression: "I have mouth cancer. It's over. I wish I could die now." Then, finally, acceptance: "Maybe I don't need my mouth."

I then collapsed into a panic nap. "Fuck, mouth cancer! Goddamnit! Should I go to the hospital now? I'm tired." I passed out for twenty minutes and woke up possessed with the anxious desire to do research. I had to confirm that what was in my mouth was cancer. I had to google mouth cancer images.

If there is a list of the shittiest ways to spend fifteen minutes, googling mouth cancer has to be right up there. I'm thinking it's number two after sticking pins in your balls for no reason. Maybe it's number one, because some people actually like sticking pins in their balls and I don't want to dismiss the BDSM community just because they are pathologically numb and have to hurt themselves to feel. Who am I to judge? I used to hit myself to get out of my head.

I looked at every mouth cancer image available and in fifteen minutes, I knew what every kind of mouth cancer looked like, but I could not find anything that looked like my mouth cancer. There were a couple of ways to interpret this. I went with "I have the rarest mouth cancer in the world. They don't even have documentation of my mouth cancer. I should take pictures of it and send it to Google so they can update their image bank, maybe name the cancer after me. Call it Oral Maronoma, it could be my legacy." I was freaking the fuck out.

Then I took some breaths and fought the urge to tweet about my mouth cancer or call my friends or go to the hospital. After feeding my need to be the unique creator of an all-new cancer, I started to work a different angle. Maybe I *didn't* have mouth cancer. It could be something else. I *am* the proud owner of a lifelong case of oral herpes, a gift I gave my ex-wife that thrills me to this day. I also get canker sores occasionally. I started to put it together and realized that what I was looking at was canker sores dyed brown by licorice. I figured it out. In that moment, when I realized what was going on, I felt like I had beaten cancer.

The next morning at 9:58 I walked out of my room with a spring in my step and a new perspective on life. I had the outlook of a survivor. A survivor of made-up mouth cancer. I stepped up to the waffle maker and made myself a lobby waffle. As I sat among the business travelers and tourist families sucking up free food I had no judgments or worries. I was elated and alive. It was the best waffle I ever tasted. I fought the urge to masturbate on the floor in front of the buffet.

20

Whole Foods

I never liked Whole Foods. I never wanted to shop there. I think it is an elitist, overpriced sham. I found Whole Foods reprehensible even before their CEO John Mackey wrote his horrible op-ed in *The Wall Street Journal*.

I hate Whole Foods because everything is overpriced. Most people want to be healthy and everybody should have access to healthy things but what Whole Foods is trying to establish and represent is the idea that you can't be healthy unless you can afford it. Notwithstanding there's no indication that organic vegetables are any better for you than non-organic vegetables. Are you worried about pesticides? You'll adapt to pesticides. What are we, a bunch of pussies all of a sudden? We've adapted to worse. The air in my house is 65 percent feline shit particulate. I can handle some non-organic fruit. In terms of nutrients they're no different. For years I shopped at a vegetable stand in Astoria from a guy with a Greek accent a block from an elevated subway that rained filth from the sky every seven minutes. I was fine.

John Mackey, the CEO of Whole Foods, wrote an editorial in *The Wall Street Journal* against health care reform. There was a lot of libertarian wrong-mindedness in his piece—some crazy ideas about tort reform, some misguided nonsense about allowing insurance companies to go across state lines, which I think will only lead to bigger monopolizations, not more competitive markets.

There's a lot of bullshit in his editorial. But the thing that interests me the most is these couple of paragraphs:

> Many promoters of health-care reform believe that people have an intrinsic ethical right to health care—to equal access to doctors, medicines and hospitals. While all of us empathize with those who are sick, how can we say that all people have more of an intrinsic right to health care than they have to food or shelter?

What I extrapolate from that paragraph is that he is willing to just let poor people die. It's not his fault or even his concern. It's part of the malignant evolutionary theory of free market capitalism. If you can't afford the good food or if you can't afford health care or if you don't have a job or if your car is dangerous because you can't get it fixed and you DIE, you just lost the game—*bzzzzz*—thanks for playing extreme capitalism.

Here's the next paragraph:

> Health care is a service that we all need, but just like food and shelter it is best provided through voluntary and mutually beneficial market exchanges. A careful reading of the Declaration of Independence and the Constitution will not reveal any intrinsic right to health care, food or shelter. That's because there isn't any. This "right" has never existed in America.

Okay, well how about we make it a new right? What's wrong with that? Later in his editorial Mackey says:

> Unfortunately many of our health-care problems are self-inflicted: two-thirds of Americans are now overweight and one-third are obese. Most of the diseases that kill us and account for about 70% of all health-care spending—heart disease, cancer, stroke, diabetes and obesity—are mostly preventable through proper diet, exercise, not smoking, minimal alcohol consumption and other healthy lifestyle choices.

So listen, all of you sick people, despite however you may have gotten ill, whether it was genetic, or who knows why you got cancer. If you just eat better, and perhaps shop at Whole Foods, you have a better shot at survival. As long as you don't get caught or killed stealing or robbing someone just to afford a head of lettuce or a slice of meat at that place, that is.

I decided to boycott Whole Foods, like lots of other people. I'd been doing it even before the editorial because it made my soul feel less dirty. But after the editorial I took it further. My subsequent action was impulsive and mysterious to me. I don't know why I did it. I will try to figure it out here.

I wanted to buy some stevia, which is a very sweet sweetener derived from a root. It has no fat in it, no chemicals. It's spectacular stuff. I usually get the stevia at Trader Joe's, a nice store that doesn't present any political or ethical dilemmas. I find TJ's irritating because everyone is so friendly and I start to question that, but that's my problem. Also, the way they package things is a little too cute for me but there are a couple of things I get there. Stevia is one of those things.

But on this day, they didn't have the stuff I wanted. The good stuff. The 100 percent pure stuff. They had the one that was cut with filler to bulk it up, like shitty cocaine.

I knew I could go to Whole Foods and get pure stevia. I'll admit I have lapses in personal integrity. I thought to myself: "You have your principles. But these are extenuating circumstances. Go get the stevia. It's not that big of a deal."

I went into the Whole Foods in Union Square in New York, which is a block away from the Trader Joe's. I'm a sellout, a scab, but I go in. I'm just going to grab the high-grade stevia. I walk into the Whole Foods and it's a cluster-fuck of food elitism, quirky handwritten signs, overpriced food, and lines and lines of people. They run people through a literal maze to pay for food. They treat you like a rodent. You have to respond to a color and a number signaling you forward like an aspirational healthy robot.

But I press on. I go downstairs, I pick up the stevia, the good shit, 100 percent. I'm holding it in my hand and looking out at the Whole Foods all around me. I'm feeling absolute disgust. I hate everything it represents. I hate John Mackey. I hate the idea that people have to pay through-the-ass exorbitant amounts of money just to have healthy food. It's not right, and I blame John Mackey, but my hatred for this kind of grotesque third-world unfairness existed before him and runs deeper than one rich asshole. I look over at the long line, the customers with their carts and baskets, penned in like cattle. I'm holding my little container of stevia. It's $7.99. I'm looking at it and realize, "Dude there is no way you are waiting on that line. And you know what? There's no way you're paying for this stevia. You cannot pay for it. What you are going to do, Marc, is you're going to hold it in your hand in front of you as if you're looking at it and walk right out of the store."

That's what I did. I held the stevia in front of me. Not because I didn't want it to look like I was stealing. I wanted to hold it right out in front of me as if to say *I'm leaving with this because I de-*

serve it, because this store sucks, because I don't want to wait on line, because the person who runs this operation is a wrong-minded, right-wing libertarian whack-job who just wants poor people to die, that's why. I was holding it as if I were the Statue of Liberty, my container of stevia my torch. I walked out through the in door, past the security guard, holding that stevia in front of me, looking at it as I walked out onto the street. When I was back out on the street, I stood in front of the store holding the plastic jar aloft. I wanted to see if anyone was going to stop me, to say, "Do you want to pay for that, buddy? Did you forget something, buddy? You're under arrest." Any of that. Nothing happened. I waited a few minutes. I probably looked ridiculous standing there on a crowded New York City street with my stevia in the air, but I waited a few minutes more and no one came. I put the stevia in my bag. I felt good.

Not only did I not feel guilty, but I felt like I wanted to go back and steal more stuff from Whole Foods. It's easy if you live in a big city. They can't manage that place. They can barely manage the lines.

Join me. Go in. Get yourself some healthy greens, some organic produce, and some vitamins if you have no money. Just bring your Whole Foods organic hemp bag, load it up, and just walk out. Walk out through the in-door. And if they ask if you paid for it just say, "Yeah, I did." Or if you pussy out, just say, "I forgot because I have a vitamin deficiency because I've been eating and shopping at affordable supermarkets lately. I should always shop here, because do you see what happens when I don't? I'm sorry," and go back in and pay for it.

Don't boycott Whole Foods—steal from them.

21

I Almost Died #3: Prince's Chicken

I am in a hotel room in Nashville, Tennessee, and things are not good inside of me. That is not an emotional observation. I don't think I'm going to die. But last night I came close. I might be being a bit dramatic. I'll let you be the judge. I put a lot of things into my body, for better or for worse. Something went in last night, and I don't know how else to say it: That thing fucked my shit up. I mean literally.

I read a short story in high school once about a hot-pepper-eating contest. I remember liking it. I don't remember much of what I was assigned to read in high school. I did a lot of sleeping in English class and my teacher was a mean old drunk woman who looked like she was balancing a pile of hair on her shaking head.

It was the descriptions of the peppers and the experience of eating them that sticks in my mind all these years later. I couldn't remember the name of the story so I googled it. It was actually hard to find. I found someone had scanned the story and put it on their personal Flickr page. Obviously, someone else at some point thought, "What was that pepper story I read in high school?"

So I reread "The Grains of Paradise," by James Street. The story turns out to be about an American man on an agricultural research mission in Mexico to learn about corn. The story culminates in a pepper-eating challenge with a local landowner and grower of peppers. The story is really about class, caste, honor, country, competition, business, and politics. I assume that's why they put the story in the book: so we could learn the power of literature to elevate and integrate layered themes into a narrative. I got none of that and I'm sure the shaking wig at the front of the class didn't illuminate any of that, but to be fair I don't remember either way. The point is: I thought it was a story about eating really hot peppers. As you get older and wiser everything becomes a bit more loaded with meaning and/or completely drained of it. It sort of happens simultaneously.

I think I was intrigued by a story about eating really hot peppers because I like things spicy. I like hot sauce. I'm not a fanatic about it but when I do find a good hot sauce I get excited. I don't search for them, which I guess is the dividing line between just liking something and being obsessed. I *have* stockpiled hot sauce in my life. Sometimes the smaller distributors go out of business and you're left hanging with the taste still in your mouth, so you had better hoard a bit if you want to get your fix. There was an amazing hot sauce called Inner Beauty with mangos and habañeros that was the shit. Gone. I held on to a bottle of that stuff for three years, doling it out sparingly. I wanted it to last forever.

I am willing to risk some discomfort for spicy food. Jalapeños destroy my stomach for a bit and cause mild to extraordinary pain when exiting my body, but I still eat them. Not as much as I used to but some part of me thinks it's still worth it. The rest of me thinks it's a problem. Anal pain and chaos does not equal feeling alive. I should learn and remember that, in all areas of my life.

When I travel, which is often, I try to find regional foods that I can't get in Los Angeles. That is really just a rationalization for me to eat barbecue, biscuits, mac and cheese, and various members of the pie family whenever I find myself anywhere that could be called southern, which means, in this country, pretty much anywhere. I always ask locals where I should eat. Then I look at the review sites to see if they check out. In Nashville almost everyone told me to go to Prince's Hot Chicken. Not necessarily because it was good but because there was nothing else like it. I was warned that it would be the hottest thing I ever put in my face.

I'm not a big fried chicken guy but I felt like everything everyone was telling me was a challenge, like they were defying me to go to Prince's. Some fans brought a cold batch of it to the show on my first night in town. I took a couple of bites. It was so hot that after two bites I started hiccupping and I thought, "I've got to get this at the source, fresh out of the fryer." But those two bites alone gave me GI tract problems the next day.

A local told me that you have to go to Prince's late at night because it's in "the hood" and it gets crazy at night. The place is open until 3 A.M. When people talk about black neighborhoods like that it implies something benignly racist. When you hear "the hood" it means someplace you wouldn't go, where you aren't wanted, but you might be tolerated and it's cool, there might be trouble, but it's cool. Oh, and black people are crazy and wild and don't live like us. Some of this is true. Some blacks don't live like me, but then some white people don't live like me, either. It's called poverty. Many poor people live in broken-down communities, and in most states, certainly in the South, some black people are kept there by layers of historic segregation, racial and economic. I am not racist but I'm a nervous person. It is not ethnicity or race specific. It is a case-by-case feeling. If I am confronted by something that I don't understand, it frightens me or makes me uncomfortable. Whether it be a person, a place, or a thing, I get nervous. I don't think that's an inappropriate human reaction. Nervousness doesn't become racism until you hear yourself saying things like "Oh, shit, there's a lot of them." Then you might need to check yourself and follow where that thought goes. You might be on a slippery slope.

I did find myself a little fascinated with black people in Tennessee. First I thought they have really great black people in Nashville. I saw them as closer to the source of what brought them here and the horror that defined them in this country in the beginning and now to varying degrees. Because of that in my mind they had more integrity. Then I was at a drugstore and I saw a black guy with a natural 'fro and in my recollection he had one of those fist picks in his back pocket. I thought, "That's a classic black guy. These are classic black people here in Nashville."

Then I thought, "Is that so different than 'Oh, shit, there's a lot of them'?"

I don't spend much time in black neighborhoods.

Not unlike a lot of creative middle-class Jewish kids, many of my heroes were black. Richard Pryor changed my life. Before I saw the first *Live in Concert* film when I was in high school, at a midnight showing with my buddy Dave, I didn't know it was possible to laugh that much. As I said before, when I first started playing guitar I became completely obsessed with learning Chuck Berry's signature opening. It changed my life. I listen to Muddy Waters frequently and have a different experience every year or so with his music. It grows deeper for me.

I was a lost kid most of my childhood and adolescence, personality-wise. I envied black identity. I envied the honesty of black expression and community. I was always alone in my mind and I certainly grew disenchanted with the Jewish thing. Black people struck me as cool and real. I thought that black people and white people were different, but the difference filled me with awe and envy.

When I graduated from college I took a train across the country. I had decided in my head that I had to ride the rails and see America drunk from a series of sleeper cars on Amtrak. My first stop was Chicago. I didn't really get out into the city but I did get my boots shined by a black guy in Union Station. He gave me a vague history of the station and I thought it was an amazing conversation. My next stop was Memphis. I spent two days there. I went to the Lorraine Motel, where Martin Luther King, Jr., was shot. I went to Graceland. I went to Beale Street, where I saw a real bluesman. Some guy called Slim sat on an old amp with a beat-up old guitar playing sloppy slide and singing incoherently. I thought it was genius. He said he knew from the way I was watching him that I was a guitar player and asked if I wanted to play while he went to the bathroom. I said hell yeah. There was a crowd gathered there. I sat down and tried to play but his guitar was tuned to some weird open tuning and I sounded awful. I sat there retuning his guitar so I could play it. He came back just as I'd finished playing half a song and he took the guitar back. He was pissed for a minute that I had screwed with his tuning but he retuned and kept playing. I stood there for more than an hour watching.

There was a small crowd gathered around. People were dancing a bit. Then this panicky-looking white man in a tie came barging through the crowd and walked up to Slim and said, "Slim, I need your amp."

Slim looked confused as he stood up and the man unplugged his guitar and started to walk away with his amp. The racially mixed crowd looked confused and started to break up. I was concerned and asked Slim what was going on. He shrugged and indicated he didn't know. So I said we should find out. So Slim and I followed the trotting man with the amp to the gate. We watched him walk into a back patio of a restaurant where there was some sort of conference going on. From outside the patio we watched the man plug a mic into Slim's amp and hand it to a guy standing at a podium. The man at the podium started talking and the guy who took the amp noticed me and Slim standing there. I was furious and demanded an explanation. The guy said, "You from around here?"

"No," I said.

"Then why don't you just mind your own business." He looked at Slim. "I'll take care of you."

In retrospect I guess the guy owned the restaurant, booked it out for an event, and didn't set up a PA. He freaked out and just took Slim's amp because he knew Slim and he knew he could. Slim probably played around there every day and was a local fixture. The guy probably threw Slim a few bucks after I wandered away defeated. It was the attitude of the whole event that angered me. I wasn't one of the Jews at the front of a civil rights march or trying to register black voters but, man, I wanted justice for Slim in the amp situation. The South might be desegregated but it may never be integrated. And by "the South" I mean America.

After a late show on Friday night in Nashville, I and a couple of other comics headed out to Prince's. We drove into the parking lot of a small strip mall. Prince's was the only storefront open. There was a three-hundred-pound man standing in front of the place wearing a tank top, smoking a cigar, and packing a sidearm. There were a few black people hanging out in front of the place. It felt like a wall of *you don't belong here*. Maybe I was projecting that. Maybe that was a wall I was creating. I just felt like an intruder, a tourist, an outsider that they put up with because the place is famous. I was nervous.

When I walked in, it was clearly a pretty beat-up joint. There were about five booths and a monitor hanging from the ceiling that looked new. On the screen there was an advertisement for advertising on that same screen. There was a pickup window in the back with handwritten menus pinned up around it. There were people just sitting around, not eating, and not looking like they were going to eat. They weren't menacing, just hanging out. There was a guy on a pay phone. You hardly ever see that anymore. It was like a community clubhouse.

I felt like I was walking into another world, chaotic and dirty but clearly an institution. There were three ways to order the chicken: medium hot, hot, and extra hot. My friend Chad told me that they would not let white people order the extra hot, which of course made me want to order it more. I was told that there was no way I could handle it. I thought to myself, "What does that even mean? Do black people have special mouths and assholes?" It seemed exclusionary. Not that we didn't deserve a little exclusion, but I was insulted. Still, I honored the myth and ordered the "hot."

There were other white people there. There were some drunk college kids and one guy who looked like a regular and going there was the high point of his life. We waited twenty minutes before they called out my number. Chad picked up the two brown paper bags of chicken. Chad's a good guy. He's been through a rough divorce and his heart is heavy; he's got a burden. That burden makes him funny. He was ecstatic to eat the chicken and to focus on the pain outside himself.

He set the bags down on the table. I pulled the wax-paper-wrapped breast out of the bag and could feel the heat on my hands. Not temperature heat but pepper heat. I was anxious about eating it. I was a little scared but I was sure I could handle it.

I took one bite of the chicken and my face started burning under my skin. My mouth was on fire. I felt like my tongue was swelling. I was sitting with five dudes who were having a conversation but the heat in my head was blurring their words. I couldn't talk or listen. I had tunnel vision. All I was thinking was "I have to get through this." Is that a way to approach food? *I've got to get through this.*

Chad was sitting next to me. He took a bite and his face turned red and he started hiccupping. He jumped up to go get water. He said he eats this all the time but he couldn't believe how hot it was. There was no relief from it. It was so hot it was beyond unnatural. It was unnecessary.

The guys started talking about someone getting arrested outside. I looked out the side of my eye. There was a black man being cuffed on the hood of a police car. There were guns drawn. I couldn't look; I was just trying to get through this thing that was happening, this holocaust in my face. I could get no relief. I was completely consumed and present in this fire in my being. It was horrible but I could not stop eating it. My eyes were watering, my body was trying to reject what I was putting into it. I was in a different dimension. It was like an amazing drug. Everything in my body was elevated, numb, and burning. All of my other senses were shutting down. I couldn't think about anything else and my whole world narrowed to the next painful bite of chicken that I seemed to have no choice but to put in my mouth. I was a gladiator of the palate. I was going to win.

When I got back to my hotel my mouth was starting to settle down. I should've found some ice cream but it was late and I just wanted to crash. I got into bed and made the mistake of touching my balls. This was the next level of the journey. A burning commenced that could not be washed off. I tried to frame it as a pleasurable sensation, a new thing that I needed to experience, but it didn't work. It just gave me a flashback to a fairly traumatic event at summer camp involving cinnamon toothpicks, crying, and an embarrassing trip to the nurse.

I was lying there in bed with the burning in my groin slowly starting to fade when I was attacked from the inside by the most profound and painful stomach cramps I had ever had. I had to curl up my body to try to ease the ache. I knew that the peppers were eating away at my stomach lining and that I would probably die of internal bleeding. I started gulping water, which worked for a minute or two. I didn't know what to do. I thought, "Wouldn't it be ironic, after all I have been through in my life, some of it in hotel rooms, to die from an overdose of hot chicken? Marc Maron found dead in hotel room. Autopsy reveals fried chicken is the culprit."

I thought about calling a cab to take me to the emergency room. Then I thought it through. I imagined the scene: me, a white guy, shows up at an emergency room in the middle of the night clutching his stomach. The admission nurse looks up at me dismissively, a judgmental arch in her eyebrow, and says, "Prince's?"

I didn't want that.

As I fell asleep I couldn't help but think I was being taught a lesson. I felt like I deserved it, like I was paying some reparation for being nervous at Prince's, for succumbing to racial mythology and not ordering the extra hot, for not getting Slim his fucking amp back from that racist restaurant owner who treated him like the help.

I rode it out. I didn't die.

★ 22 ★

Xenophobia, Autoerotic Asphyxiation, and the History of Irish Poetry

Running away works. Sometimes you have to change it up: new people, new restaurants, new Laundromat, new barista, new life. Yeah, the adage is true—that wherever you go, there you are—but you in an entirely new setting is a new you, or at least the old you in a new context, and that's not nothing.

That is why I've grown to like the road. There is a freedom that comes through the loneliness of being stranded by work in another town or country. My freedom initially takes the form of self-abuse of some kind: food, sex, masturbation, drugs, making a mess, or oversleeping. My impulse: "I can make this mess here. It doesn't count. This is planet road."

I am a homeowner, which means that a good part of my brain is always consumed with all the little anxieties and tasks that go along with owning a home, a list too long to make here without afflicting myself with paralyzing stress. The minute I walk into a clean hotel room and realize that I am not responsible for anything other than not destroying it, all my other worries melt away.

I hook up my computer, see what the room has to offer (a special shower fixture, a view), and sit down in my temporary furnished box and relax on a strange, expertly made bed. I then lie down on that bed and masturbate.

As real-life anxieties melt away, my suddenly free mind starts to piece together everything that led up to me being in that hotel room. Within a few hours I land on the question, "Who am I, really? No one knows me. Do I know myself?" That's when I go outside, untethered from my life, and start shopping around—for love or at least a functional identity.

That can be hard depending on where the hotel is located. Downtown areas usually suck because after five they are ghost towns and you just become a lone stranger wandering around wondering if you are going to be murdered in the street or if anyone else is alive in this city and if so where are they. University towns are okay, for a few hours, before you realize that you are old and silly. I try to seek out places that make me feel connected: coffee shops, record stores, hipster blocks, malls (ironically), indigenous food. Anything that will connect me to other people, a culture, life. I want to do what locals do. I am living there for a few days. I can also justify just about anything as professional research. I have to try new things so I can make them funny.

Running away works, but it doesn't work as well for me abroad. I am a little xenophobic. It's not limited to other countries or people from other cultures. I can feel out of place standing in my driveway. I feel that way with my neighbors. I feel that way at the Mexican supermarket down the street. The feeling is just compounded when I am in another country.

On a recent trip to Glasgow, Scotland, I was determined not to freak out about being in another country. As an American I am always threatened by smaller, culturally well-defined countries.

The Scottish have a cultural identity that has lasted centuries. They have different cereals, cakes, and brands. Everything is really old. I convinced myself that it would be fine, that they'd get me. They speak English, after all. That turned out to be arguable.

But I decided to enter Glasgow without fear, and within hours I was feeling very comfortable. The Scots I came in contact with were nothing but pleasant. The audiences were great. I felt like I was turning a corner on my feelings of awkwardness and loneliness abroad. I did *Scorching the Earth*, the big divorce show I put together after I went through that horrible time in my life. I was nervous about it because *Scorching* is devoted to a single story; one that runs through a lot of painful stuff. I had a hard enough time doing it in the States. But the Glaswegians were a great audience. I realized that there's a different tradition to comedy here. There is a storytelling tradition in the United Kingdom. They can listen to jokes and they like jokes, but they can also be completely compelled by a longer story, even without the constant payoff in punch lines you get with a series of loosely connected jokes. It was so refreshing and encouraging. It was the best performance of that show I had ever done.

My first morning there I got up and went to the complimentary breakfast buffet off the lobby. They had sausages and things I had never seen before. Blood pudding, black pudding, haggis patties, sausage links, thick-cut English bacon, Lorne sausage, which is a square patty of what seemed to be deep-fried particle meat. I wanted to eat them all. I couldn't have been more excited to cram what they call the square sausage right into my face. I ate a little bit of all this stuff. I had heard about haggis but I had never eaten it before. I was still frightened of that. I only took a little taste of it but I couldn't intellectually overcome what it is—lamb's heart, liver, lungs, and suet. For some reason I could eat the black pudding with no problem and loved it. I guess coagulated blood was simpler to wrap my head around. The point was, I wanted to eat like a local. I wanted to be accepted there, even on the inside. I shoved it all into my face hole.

I then went walking around Glasgow smelling the air around me and thinking, "Are they frying food everywhere here?" And then I realized the smell was coming off me. I was sweating broken-down animal fat for two days. That night I woke up thinking there was somebody else in my bed, perhaps an animal trainer or farmer, then I realized it was me. It smelled weird. I thought this must be what it is like to be Scottish on the inside.

I talked to a Glaswegian and asked, "Do you eat this way every day, because if this is the way you do it, I'm going to try. I'm going to run with you."

"Of course we don't eat that every day. What do you think, we're fucking stupid?" he said.

"Well, how do you it?" I asked, slightly desperate.

He told me that the Lorne sausage is a quick-breakfast type of food that is usually ordered as a sausage sandwich served on a roll, along with a potato scone, which is like a pancake or a piece of chapati bread.

I looked up Lorne sausage on Wikipedia to find out what part of Scottish history I was digesting. I learned that it's a brick of ground-up pig cut with a little bit of Rusk filler. After I ate it, later in the day, I talked to another guy about it and he said you put it on a roll and top it with ketchup or tomato chutney. I asked about mustard and he said you would never put mustard on that, so I felt like an idiot. I had to fight the urge to do it all again with ketchup. I just couldn't handle it anymore. The next day I ate some muesli and fruit instead. I'd had enough.

That didn't stop me that night from wandering alone into a curry shop looking to reward myself for a good show. This is another lesson that I learned about the United Kingdom. I'm used to eating Middle Eastern or Indian food in America. You order a kebab, you get one kebab. So I went in and ordered two shish kebabs and some pakoras and they gave me three mountains of food in Styrofoam cases—tandoori chicken, kebabs smothered in onions and a syrupy, sugary sauce, and a whole box of pakoras. I shoveled it all into my hole.

I think it should be known that I have an eating disorder that involves intense shame over eating almost anything. The muesli wasn't enough to erase that deep guilt. Alone again in my room I felt stranded, fat, and wrong. Because I was thinking about fat, I started thinking about how I hadn't gone to the gym in months, and even though I had my running shoes with me, I hadn't actually worn them yet. My New Balances have been around the world, but they don't get out much. I looked at my running shoes on the floor. I looked at my computer on the desk. I knew porn was just two clicks away. And I thought: Am I going to be that guy? Am I going to sit in my room in shame masturbating and napping?

In that moment I really understood how David Carradine hung himself while he was masturbating in a hotel room on the road. Because is that something you can do at home? I don't think so. That's a hotel room thing, hanging yourself with a belt off a closet door while you jerk off. Why would anyone do that at home? Many times sitting in a hotel room somewhere I've thought, "I want to kill myself." Then, within a few minutes I think, "Fuck it, I'll jerk off." I suppose combining the two, cheating one to amplify the other, would make perfect sense eventually. I'm not saying I'd do it. I don't want to risk my life masturbating. I am saying it crossed my mind sitting there in Scotland sweating slightly curried lard on a strange bed. I'm glad I didn't know the procedure and I had forgotten my belt. I settled for masturbating and napping. Then I put on my running shoes and walked around Glasgow. I didn't run but I wanted them to get out.

Ireland was another challenge for me. I've got to be honest with you. I used to have an aversion to Irish people. This was back when I was in college. I lived in Boston, so I guess my problem was specifically with American Irish people. I felt that they were all out to get me. It all revolved around a traffic incident.

I remember the day; it was the day John Belushi died. I was devastated. I was driving around in my car, in grief. One of my favorite comedians was dead. I got pulled over. The officer's name was O'Brien. I don't remember why he pulled me over, but I didn't have a current insurance card so they towed my car and sent me home.

I remember O'Brien looking at my license and expired insurance card and saying, "You can't drive this vehicle."

"Okay, I'll drive it home and I won't drive until I get my new insurance card. I promise."

"No, you can't drive it at all. Get out now. I am having it towed."

"John Belushi is dead," I said.

"Get out of the vehicle."

I stood at the side of the road, sad, with the name O'Brien ringing in my ears. O'Brien, O'Brien, O'Brien. With every angry repetition, the voice in my head spoke with a thicker brogue until it sounded like the evil leprechaun in those horror movies. *O'Brien.* All it took was one O'Brien to make me feel like the Irish were against me and had been for centuries. Officer O'Brien sparked a several-year-long paranoia.

I had to go to some sort of arraignment to get the ticket dismissed and O'Brien was there. I was before a magistrate of some kind; let's say his name was Malloy. I told them I got my insurance back. They looked at me and Malloy said he'd let me off because this coming Sunday was Easter Sunday. Then O'Brien looked at me and said, "Yeah, it's Passover, too."

From that point I got a little uncomfortable around the Irish. I'd go to bars and have too much to drink and think there was an Irish conspiracy to take me down. I was a pretty sensitive guy and I was a Jew. There was a type of Irish townie in New England that scared the shit out of me. They just liked to fight for fighting's sake and they were menacing. I found them threatening but I also envied them in a slightly condescending way because they seemed to know exactly who they were. They were angry, usually wasted, and clearly not without issues, but they were consistent in their disposition and seemed to have full, active social lives, mostly revolving around terrorizing college students and being thrown in jail for being drunk and disorderly. I respected their spirit. In my mind they were a rugged, tough bunch that got shit done and weren't afraid. My opposites.

I made a tremendous faux pas years later while interviewing the author Roddy Doyle on a radio show. It revealed a racism that I had not really thought through. Someone had told me an Irish joke that I thought was a perfect representation of what I respected about the Irish in a general way, that rugged spirit and determinism. I told the joke to him to his face, excited:

During the westward expansion two Irish immigrants landed in New York City. They went to a bar and asked the bartender if there was any work available. The bartender told them to head west because they were offering a dollar for every Indian scalp brought in. The two Irish guys headed west and went looking for Indians.

They found themselves riding through a ravine and all
of a sudden hundreds of Indians started lining up along
the top of the ravine on both sides preparing to descend
on the two Irishmen. They stopped their horses and
looked around at all of the Indians. One said to the
other, "Look at all those Indians. We're going to be
rich."

Roddy Doyle indulged me in the telling and, when I was
through, quietly stared at me. I laughed alone and then we both
entered an awkward silence once it occurred to me that he hated
the joke, and probably me. I thought the joke was a great charac-
terization of the Irish spirit. I never even entertained the idea that
the two men in the joke were morons. I just thought they were
ambitious and fearless and part of me thought they might pull it
off.

The first time I went to Ireland was in 1999. I was recently divorced for the first time and newly sober. I don't want to be hack-
neyed about it but people drink in Ireland. That is a reality.
Sobriety is almost a mortal sin there, but that's where I went to
flaunt my recovery. I felt alienated and alone, rejected by the entire country. I remember going to AA meetings there, five of us
huddled together in a church in a castle. That was nice. But there
was a fortressed feeling about it. Like we were prisoners of rare
blood and needed protection. Both are actually true.

I spent two trying weeks in Kilkenny performing for a half-
rural, half-suburban Irish crowd who were not necessarily comedy fans. They were there for the festival. I would assume many of
them went to comedy shows once a year. It didn't go very well. I
just don't think my introspection and personal struggle could

compete with what I believed was a history of oppression. The Irish people had been through enough and whatever I was going on about seemed like indulgence. I even realized that.

It was a projection on my part. My brain seeks to make me unique even if it's in a bad light. I scared myself into thinking I was alone and being judged by Ireland as a weak, whiny, gutless Jew with problems.

I still loved being in Ireland. I was shocked at how beautiful the place is. The intensity of the colors and the damp clarity of the landscapes are really stunning. I was moved in a deep way. And no matter what Roddy Doyle thought of my joke, I still respected the land and the people. Kilkenny was one of the most gorgeous places I have ever been but there was a heaviness beneath the beauty, the weight of history and the hardship that you can feel everywhere. But that potential darkness is countered by the lightness of the Irish approach to life—their cheerful embrace of the tragic and their slightly drunken acceptance of the way things are—that levels it out. My shows weren't very good there and I was still slightly afraid of my audience and I left feeling defeated, but when I had the opportunity ten years later to go back, I jumped at it.

When I got there for the second time I started every day with a run that took me right by Kilkenny Castle, which is big and old and glorious to look at. I knew nothing about it beyond that, but I took that beautiful run every morning past that castle and thought it was awe-inspiring; someone important must have lived there. Probably many important people lived there, important relative to the history of Ireland, or maybe not important at all, just kind of powerful. Either way it was pretty. It turns out that the castle was built in 1195. Eleven ninety-five! My house was built in 1924 and it's about to slide down a fucking hill. It turns out that it's possible to build a wall out of rock and basic mortar that will last a thousand years. As an American, that's shocking.

The run along the river was keeping me sane while I was there.

The air is so clean, maybe because of all the green, all the trees and plants, the relentless lushness everywhere. But it's so damn clean. I was running along a river next to the castle and listening to the Rolling Stones. I thought, "What the fuck is wrong with me?" Here I was running through the freshest air, the cleanest atmosphere I've been in all my life, and I've got the Rolling Stones blaring in my head. So I turned the music off and pulled the earphones out and just listened to the water and my breath and watched the Irish scenery.

I was a better comic than I was on my first trip and I rose above my fear of Irish antipathy to eventually have some good sets there. I felt like I had finally put my Irish complex to rest, which freed me to enjoy my time there. Then I had a moment the last night I was there which I call "The History of Irish Poetry," a better representation of the Irish character than the joke about the Indians.

It was very late, around three-thirty in the morning. I was walking down the empty streets of Kilkenny with another comic. There was a full moon. We had just left a wrap party for the comedy festival. The streets were so quiet we could hear our feet hitting the uneven cobblestones beneath us. It was a perfect night. All the pubs had closed and you could feel history haunting the ominous darkened rock walls that lined the street.

Out of nowhere a man appeared in the middle of the street like an apparition. He was a large man, fat with a white shirt. He was sweaty and his face was all red. He was holding a half-filled pint glass of beer. I had no idea where it came from. There were no open pubs around. When we saw him we stopped some distance away, warily, like we had come upon a wild animal. He stopped, too, looked right at us, raised the glass up, and exuberantly shouted, "It's good to be happy!" Then, without missing a beat, he lowered the glass and lowered his head and said, almost under his breath, "There's no hope."

The history of Irish poetry.

Googleheimers

My mother lives in Florida so I visit there at least once a year. I used to hate Florida, until I realized it is a great American freak show. It is the most densely populated peculiar state I have been in. It is filled with people either at the end of their lives or the end of their ropes.

The old people are interesting; they are finally free to do whatever they want but don't quite have the energy to do it, yet they aren't letting that stop them. Combine that with the odd mix of locals. I don't want to call them rednecks or hill people, but you get it. There's a little taste of the South in the worst way possible. There's also a large Latino community.

It's a full-on, densely populated, always humid, senior salsa hillbilly hoedown all the time down here. The roads are very exciting because you just never know if someone is drunk or old or learned how to drive in another country.

On my recent visits I've become a bit concerned with my empathy for the elderly. As I get older I'm losing the excitement about talking to them and engaging with them that I had when I was younger, when they seemed so wise and interesting. Maybe as I'm approaching old age myself—and I feel something happening to my brain—I am pulling away from the old people out of my own fear. In any case, I find myself wishing that somehow we could put all these old people down there to some productive use. The spirit of that thought illustrates a serious lack of empathy, but here we go.

I had a fairly revolutionary idea. I don't know if it's doable. I want to call it Googleheimers. Maybe it's wrong-minded but let me explain. Florida is riddled with huge condo complexes with literally thousands of senior citizens in them. We need to create an interface that allows people to get on their computers and access all the wisdom and stories of the old people in the condo developments through a search engine. I'm not a technological guy so I don't know how you would go about doing this. I'm trying with my limited knowledge to figure out how to make this work without the need to implant some sort of chip in their heads. That seems a bit totalitarian and wrong but it might be necessary. Maybe it could be pitched as some form of medical alert device. At their next doctor's appointments doctors could talk to them about implanting a chip in their brains that would hook them up to a new service. If anything goes wrong with their health the chip will automatically dispatch an ambulance or generate a phone call with lifesaving information. The chip should actually do this. We have the technology, right?

When confronted with this new lifesaving technology they might respond with some version of "What? I don't understand. A machine?"

"It's not going to hurt," the doctor will say. "And you'll never need to call the ambulance. It will just come."

There should be a representative from Googleheimers present to tell the prospective source brain, "Also, people will be able to see into your brain when they search for information, like events in history and whatnot. You'd be helping."

"I don't think I want to."

"We'll give you a break on your medicine if you let us put it in."

"All right. I'm not going to feel anything, right?"

"Nope, painless."

"Okay, go ahead and put the gizmo in. I'm on a lot of medicine."

There should also be a video element. Maybe in every apartment there's a camera. When somebody Googleheimers something that the particular person in this apartment knows, maybe a little swing music or doo-wop plays and a light comes on to signal to the resident that they need to go to their computer.

Let's say you Googleheimer the JFK assassination. All of a sudden a little light goes off in Murray Jacobs's condo and the music comes on. He sits up at his little portable TV dinner table and says, "Oh no, here we go." He goes and sits down at his computer and the camera comes on. He sees "JFK assassination" on his screen and starts reflecting about it to you. So you're looking for information and boom, there's Murray saying, "Oh sure, I remember. That was a sad day. We'd eaten lunch at the place on Seventh Avenue, me and Doris. We heard the thing about the guy—Kennedy. We liked him even though he was Catholic. He was a nice-looking guy. He seemed like he liked the right things. He liked the black people. We were very, I don't know what you call it today; we didn't call it liberal back then, we just called it being a good person. Then we heard the news and it was awful. Doris cried a little bit and we took home half of the cheesecake and I think I had diarrhea because of it. That's what I remember."

That would be the type of information you get when you search Googleheimers. You can use it in a term paper or perhaps for a speaking engagement. You could quote Murray, for example, if you were writing a paper for school: "This was an awful day in

November 1963, according to Murray Jacobs. It was sad and they didn't finish their cheesecake and he got diarrhea."

I think that would be entertaining information, sourced to someone who lived through it. It would run the range of people who were at the retirement community. However, I'm thinking I should change the name because Googleheimers might be considered a little derogatory, with its Semitic overtones. The name SeniorMatrix might be more fitting.

★ 24 ★

Cooking at Thanksgiving

I prepare a yearly Thanksgiving dinner for twenty-four people at my mother's house in Florida. It is a healing and horrifying event for me, full of joy and spite. My mother taught me to be afraid of food. Not all food, but certainly all foods with sugar and fat in them, so almost all food. I think the first word I was taught by my mother was *mommy* and the second word was *skinny*. Counting calories was how I learned to do math. My mother has been 116 pounds for as long as I can remember. Needless to say, she is an awful cook because she doesn't eat anything that normal people would want to eat.

I like to cook. I didn't learn much in college but I did learn to appreciate cooking. I had a philosophy professor who threw awesome parties at his house. He was one of those borderline inappropriate teachers full of menace, intelligence, and sexuality and he was a gourmet cook. At one of his soirées I asked how he learned to cook and he said by reading cookbooks. Then he hit on me. That's it! I was inspired—not to be gay but to learn how to cook. The idea that I could do something giving and seemingly selfless for a group of people and still be the center of attention seemed like a magical talent. I wanted to cook for people—or "at" people, as a recent girlfriend accused me of doing. It all made sense. I wanted to cook at my mother for making me crazy.

Of course I cook with spite. That is part of my creativity as a comic and an amateur chef. Armed with a knack for recipes and a vengeance against my mother, I started the tradition of traveling from wherever I lived—New York, Los Angeles—to Hollywood, Florida, to cook *at* my mother and *for* my extended family.

Every year I get to her house a few days before Thanksgiving and start stocking up. Fresh-killed turkey, turkey parts, potatoes (sweet and regular), cream, sour cream, whipping cream, butter, sugar, flour. I fill my mother's fridge with some of her mortal enemies. She deals with it. She likes having me there once a year. She even has her one knife sharpened and borrows a carving set.

I refuse her help and I mock her questions.

"Can't we use low-fat sour cream?"

"No."

"Why don't you use half the butter?"

"What's the point? This is once a year."

"Will you make a few brussels sprouts without butter?"

"Fine. I can do that. Now leave me alone. I am cooking."

The stuffing is the key to my Thanksgiving dinner. It is a recipe passed down to me from my college professor. It is rich and mind-blowing. It is memorable. It makes an impact. It is talked about. I cook the stuffing outside the bird.

Last Thanksgiving, in the crucial moments before serving the meal, I put the stuffing in the oven in the condo next door to brown the top. Mom's neighbors are snowbirds and we use their condo for a second oven. She has the keys. I ran back to my mom's to strain the brussels sprouts. I went back next door to a smoke-filled kitchen. I pulled the stuffing out. It was black and smolder-ing. I stormed back to my mother's and said, "We're screwed. Everything is ruined. Send everyone home." She came back with me to the other condo. I paced around screaming, "What's the point, let's throw it away, the whole dinner is destroyed!" My mother said, "Scrape the burnt stuff off the top. Stop making a production."

I wanted to make a production, The "Marc's Thanksgiving Dinner Is Perfect" production. I do every year and now my lead actor was a mess and might not be able to perform.

"What do you know about food? Who is going to eat this? Look at it!"

"So what?" she said. "You're being a baby."

I was. I pulled all the charred stuffing off and I put out the food. No one seemed to notice. The dinner was a hit.

My mother sat there with her plate of plain brussels sprouts and some of the black stuffing top.

"You know what, Marc? The burnt top is the best part."

I guess my mother loves me.

★ 25 ★

The Montreal
Just for Laughs Comedy
Festival Keynote Address

I was asked to give the keynote speech at the 2011 Just for Laughs Comedy Festival in Montreal. I was nervous and horrified as I approached the podium at 1 P.M. on July 28, 2011, in front of about four hundred peers and show-biz types. These were people who I felt judged me my entire career. People who I thought had kept me down and made my life difficult. But once I stopped at the podium a peace came over me. I knew that what I was about to say was from my heart. I knew there were some laughs and some pain. I knew that I had arrived . . . in my body. I fought back some tears a few minutes in but I got through it. It was one of the most intense and elating experiences of my life. I showed up for myself and my craft.

Welcome to the Montreal Just for Laughs Comedy Festival and fuck you, some of you; you know who you are. Wait. Sorry. That was the old me. I would like to apologize for being a dick just

then. Goddamnit. See, that's progress. The amount of time between action and apology was seconds.

I am excited to be here. So I will now proceed to make this
speech all about me and see where that takes us.

Things are going pretty well for me right now and that is a
problem. I don't know what kind of person you are but I am the
kind of person who when things are going well there is a voice in
my head saying, "You're going to fuck it up. You're going to fuck
it up, Marc." Over and over and over again. I just wish that voice
were louder than the voice screaming, "Let's fuck it up! Come on,
pussy! What happened to you? Fuck it up. Burn some bridges,
fuck up your career, fuck up this speech, break up with your girlfriend, start drinking again, pussy! You used to have balls and
edge! Have you forgotten what it's like being alone on a couch
drunk and crying with no future and nothing left to lose? Have
you forgotten what freedom feels like, pussy? Fuck it up!"

So, that is going on right now.

When they asked me to give this speech months ago the first
thing I said to my manager was "What? They can't get anyone
else? With this much time? Really?" Then my manager said,
"They want you." So I asked, "Why me?"

Why ask why me? is the better question. This was obviously a
good thing—I got the gig—but I'm the kind of person that needs
to deconstruct even a good thing so I can understand what is
expected of me and who is expecting it. You would think, "Well,
Marc, they want you to be funny." Not good enough. In my mind
I needed to know what the angle was. Did no one else want to do
this? Did someone drop out? Be honest, who said no already?
Chelsea Handler? Did Chelsea Handler say no already? I don't
want Chelsea Handler's sloppy seconds. Am I cheap? I mean, shit,

I've been doing comedy for twenty-five years and I've been invited to this festival maybe twice before this. Which is ridiculous considering how many "new faces" I've tried out along the way. To their credit the festival did have me on the "remember these old faces" show a few years ago, but I get it. Let's be honest. I haven't made anyone in this room any real money. I'm currently working out of my garage. I am in a constant battle with resentment against many people in this room. So, again, why me?

You see what happened there? Within minutes the opportunity to give this speech became "This is a setup. They're fucking me. What kind of bullshit is this?"

That is the kind of thinking that has kept me out of the big time for my entire career.

Okay, I'm going to try to address both sides here—the industry and the comics. It's not really an *us against them* situation but sometimes it feels like it is.

As I said, I have been doing stand-up for twenty-five years. I've put more than half my life into building my clown. That's how I see it. Comics keep getting up onstage and in time the part of them that lives and thrives up there is their clown. My clown was fueled by jealousy and spite for most of my career. I'm the clown who recently read *The War for Late Night* and thought it was basically about me not being in show business. I'm the clown who thought most of Jon Stewart's success was based on his commitment to a haircut. I'm the clown that thought Louis C.K.'s show *Louie* should be called *Fuck You, Marc Maron*.

Three years ago my clown was broke, on many levels, and according to my manager at the time, unbookable and without options. That was a good talk:

My manager: Nobody wants to work with you. I can't get you an agent. I can't you get you any road work. I can't get you anything.

Me: Uh, okay, so, uh, what do we do . . .

My manager: Are you looking at my hair? Why are you looking at my hair? Does it look bad?

Me: No, it's fine. What should I do?

My manager: I don't know what we're going to do. Stop looking at my hair. Am I fat? Seriously, am I?

My first thought after that meeting was: "I'm going to kill myself." My second thought was: "I could get a regular job." My third thought was: "I need a new manager." I think I had the order wrong. I drove home defeated. Twenty-five years in and I had nothing. I was sitting alone in my garage in a house I was about to lose because of that bitch—let's not get into that now—and I realized, "Fuck, *you can build a clown, and they might not come.*" I was thinking, "It's over. It's fucking over." Then I thought: "You have no kids, no wife, no career, certainly no plan B. Why not kill yourself?" I thought about suicide a lot—not because I really wanted to kill myself. I just found it relaxing to know that I could if I had to.

Then I thought maybe I could get a regular job. Even though the last regular job I had was in a restaurant like twenty-five years ago. I said to myself, *I still got it! It's like riding a bike. Just get me a spatula and watch me flip some eggs or some burgers.* Then I thought, "What, are you fucking crazy? You think they're going to hire a forty-seven-year-old man whose last restaurant job was part-time short order cook in 1987? How are you going to explain those lost years? Are you going to show the bar manager your *Conan* reel? You're an idiot."

Broke, defeated, and careerless, I started doing a podcast in that very garage where I was planning my own demise. I started talking about myself on the mic with no one telling me what I could or couldn't say. I started to reach out to comics. I needed help. Personal help. Professional help. Help. I needed to talk. So I reached out to my peers and talked to them. I started to feel better about life, comedy, creativity, community. I started to understand who I was by talking to other comics and sharing it with you. I started to laugh at things again. I was excited to be alive. Doing the podcast and listening to comics was saving my life. I realized *that* is what comedy can do for people.

You know what the industry had to do with that?

Absolutely nothing.

When I played an early episode for my now former manager in his office, thinking that I was turning a career corner and we finally had something, he listened for three minutes and said, "I don't get it."

I don't blame him. Why would he? It wasn't on his radar or in his wheelhouse. There's no package deal, no episode commitment, no theaters to sell out. He had no idea what it was or how to extract money from it *and* I did it from my garage. Perfect. It took me twenty-five years to do the best thing I had ever done and there was no clear way to monetize it.

I'm ahead of the game.

So, back to the offer for this speech. I thought *wait,* that's the reason they want me—I do this podcast out of my garage that has had over twenty million downloads in less than two years. It is critically acclaimed. I have interviewed over two hundred comics, created live shows, I am writing a book, I have a loyal borderline-obsessive fan base who bring me baked goods and artwork, I have evolved as a person and a performer, I am at the top of my game and no one can tell me what to do—I built it myself, I work for myself, I have full creative freedom.

I am the future of show business. Not your show business, my show business. They want me to do this speech because I am the future of our industry.

Then my *new* manager got back to me and said, "They liked the jokes you did when you introduced Kindler a couple of years ago. That's why they asked you."

So, it was the jokes about them, you, the industry, that got them interested. Hmm. Fuck. That was like two jokes. I'm not good at insult comedy. Any time I do roast types of jokes they go too far, cut too deep, too true, get me in trouble.

I think the president of Comedy Central, Doug Herzog, is still mad at me. I would like to take this opportunity to apologize again to Doug. Years ago, when Doug Herzog and Eileen Katz first moved to Comedy Central from MTV and began retooling it, I performed at a Comedy Central party at Catch A Rising Star. I remember the joke I did. I said, "I am glad that Doug and Eileen moved from MTV to Comedy Central because I think that all television should look like a twenty-four-hour, round-the-clock pie-eating contest." I don't know if it was the venom I said it with or what, but two days later I was in Eileen Katz's office with my old manager, who was having a great hair day, apologizing to Eileen for that joke. So, I am not the guy to make you industry people laugh at yourselves. Kindler will do that in a couple of days. And if I could, in the spirit of making an amends, I would like to apologize to Doug Herzog, again, and say I am sorry, Doug. Since you have been there, Comedy Central has become the best pie-eating contest on television.

Yes, I have been bitter in my life. I have felt slighted by the industry and misunderstood. I have made mistakes and fucked things up. That's the kind of comic I am. It isn't unusual. I will admit and accept my faults and mistakes but it bothers me that the industry takes comics for granted and makes us jump through stupid hoops and lies to us—constantly. I get it. You think it's part of your job but how about a little respect for us—the commodity. The clowns.

When I was a kid watching comedians on TV and listening to their records they were the only ones that could make it all seem okay. They seemed to cut through the bullshit and disarm fears and horror by being clever and funny. I don't think I could have survived my childhood without watching stand-up comics. When I started doing comedy I didn't understand show business. I just wanted to be a comedian. Now, after twenty-five years of doing stand-up and the last two years of having long conversations with over two hundred comics I can honestly say they are some of the most thoughtful, philosophical, open-minded, sensitive, insightful, talented, self-centered, neurotic, compulsive, angry, fucked-up, sweet, creative people in the world.

I love comedians. I respect anyone who goes all in to do what I consider a noble profession and art form. Despite whatever drives us toward this profession—insecurity, need for attention, megalomania, poor parenting, anger, a mixture of all the above—whatever it is, we comics are out there on the front lines of our sanity.

We risk all sense of security and the possibility of living stable lives to do comedy. We are out there in B rooms, dive bars, coffee shops, bookstores, and comedy clubs trying to find the funny, trying to connect, trying to interpret our problems and the world around us and make them into jokes. We are out there dragging our friends and coworkers to comedy clubs at odd hours so we can get onstage. We are out there desperately tweeting, updating statuses, and shooting silly videos. We are out there driving ten hours straight to feature in fill-in-the-blank-city-here. We are out there acting excited on local morning radio programs with hosts whose malignant egos are as big as their regional popularity. We are out there pretending we like club owners and listening to their "input." We are out there fighting the good fight against our own weaknesses: battling courageously with Internet porn, booze, pills, weed, blow, hookers, hangers-on, sad, angry girls we can't get out of our room, Twitter trolls, and broken relationships. We are out there on treadmills at Holiday Inn Expresses and Marriott suite hotels trying to balance out our self-destructive compulsions, sadness, and fat. We are up making our own waffles at 9:58 A.M., two minutes before the free buffet closes, and thrilled about it. Do not underestimate the power of a lobby waffle to change your outlook.

All this for what? For the opportunity to be funny in front of as many people as possible and share our point of view, entertain, tell some jokes, crunch some truths, release some of the tension that builds up in people, in the culture and ourselves.

So, if I could I would like to help out some of the younger comics here with some things that I learned from experience in show business. Most of these only refer to those of us that have remained heatless for most of our careers. I can't speak to heat. I do know that symbiosis with the industry is necessary after a certain point and there are great agents, managers, and executives who want to make great product but for the most part it's about money. To quote a promoter who was quoting an older promoter in relation to his involvement with the Charlie Sheen tour: "Don't smell it, sell it." True story.

The list.

1. Show business is not your parents. When you get to Hollywood you should have something more than "Hey! I'm here! When do we go on the rides?"
2. Try to tap into your authentic voice, your genuine funny, and build from there.
3. Try to find a manager that gets you.

4. Nurturing and developing talent is no longer relevant. Don't expect it. If you want to hear about that, talk to an agent, manager, or comic from back in the day . . . but don't get sucked in. They'll pay for the meal but they'll feed on your naiveté to fuel their diminishing relevance and that can be a soul suck.

5. If you have a manager there is a language spoken by them and their assistants that you should begin to understand. For example, when an assistant says "He's on a call" or "I'll try to get her in the car" or "He just stepped out" or "I don't have her right now" or "They're in a meeting" or "He's at lunch" or "She's on set" or . . . all of those mean: They've got no time for you. You have nothing going on. Go make something happen so they can take credit for it.

6. Sometimes a "general meeting" just means that executives had an open day, needed to fill out their schedule, and want to be entertained. Don't get your hopes up.

7. If your manager says any of these: "We're trading calls" or "I have a call in to them" or "They said you killed it" or "They love you" or "They're having a meeting about you" or "We're waiting to hear back" or "They're big fans" . . . these usually mean: You didn't get it and someone will tell you secondhand.

8. There is really no business like show business. Except maybe prostitution. There's a bit of overlap there.

9. This is not a meritocracy. Get over yourself.

10. Dave Rath will be your manager.

The amazing thing about being a comedian is that no one can tell us to stop even if we should. Delusion is necessary to do this. Some of you aren't that great. Some of you may get better. Some of you are great . . . now. Some of you may get opportunities even when you stink. Some of you will get them and they will go no-where and then you have to figure out how to buffer that disap-pointment and because of that get funnier or fade away. Some of you may be perfectly happy with mediocrity. Some of you will get nothing but heartbreak. Some of you will be heralded as geniuses and become huge. Of course, all of you think that one describes you . . . hence the delusion necessary to push on. Occasionally everything will sync up and you will find your place in this racket. There is a good chance it will be completely surprising and not anything like you expected.

I'm not a household name, I'm not a huge comic, I have not made millions of dollars, but I am okay and I make a living. I'm good with that. Finally. Comedy saved my life but also destroyed it in many ways. That is the precarious balance of our craft and some of us don't survive it. We lost a few truly great comics this year.

Greg Giraldo isn't here, which is weird. He was always here. Greg was a friend of mine and of many of yours. He wasn't a close friend but we were connected by the unspoken bond between comics. After talking to hundreds of comics I know that bond runs deeper than just friendship and is more honest than most relationships. He certainly was a kindred spirit. I battle demons every day and as of today, I am winning, or at least have a détente. Greg lost that fight. He was a brilliant comedian but in a way that is rare. He was not a dark, angry cloud. He was smart, current, honest, courageous, and did it with humility and light. He was a comedic force of nature that is profoundly missed. He was just a guy that always seemed so alive that accepting that he isn't is hard and sad. He is survived by his ex-wife, his kids, and his YouTube videos. We miss him.

In an interesting twist this year, Robert Schimmel did not die of cancer but he did pass. Bob was a class act. A legacy to true-blue lounge comedy and an impeccable craftsman of the story and the joke. He battled a horrible disease for over a decade and brought a lot of laughs and hope to people affected by cancer. He made me laugh—a lot. I listen to his CDs if I need a real laugh. That is as honest a tribute as I can give. I miss him and I am sad I didn't get to talk to him more.

Mike DeStefano as a person went through more shit than I can even imagine. Some of it self-generated, all of it tragic and mind-blowing, and he overcame it. How? With comedy. I recently talked to his brother, Joe, who said, "Mike had a tough time living until he found comedy, and then it was the opposite. Doing comedy is what saved him. His comedy helped a lot of people and it helped him." I'd never met a guy more at peace with his past and present and more excited about a future that sadly isn't going to happen now, but he knew in his heart he was living on borrowed time and every day was a gift.

All of these guys should have had many more years of life between them but they didn't. These guys were unique in that they were real comics, hilarious, deep, hard-core, risk-taking, envelope-pushing artists that made a profound impact on people and changed minds and lives with their funny. I know that to be true.

I'm not sure if there is one point to this speech or any, really. If you are a comic, hang in there if you can, because you never know what's going to happen or how it is going to happen and there are a lot more ways and places for it to happen. I know my place in show business now. It's in my garage. Who knows where yours is but there is truly nothing more important than comedy. . . . Well, that may be an overstatement. There are a few things more important than comedy but they aren't funny . . . until we make them funny.

Godspeed. Have a good festival. We're good, right?

Epilogue: Boomer Lives!

The day I started taping my TV show for IFC called *Maron*, my cat Boomer disappeared. It was a monumental day. On some level I had been working toward it my entire life. Everything was changing for me. What I had invested my whole life into was coming to fruition, and on my own terms. I walked into my back-yard to feed him and he wasn't there. There was a crazy stray out there but no Boomer. So I fed the stray. Maybe he would go give Boomer the heads-up on the food. I also thought the stray might have had something to do with Boomer's disappearance. They had been fighting. But then again, he'd been coming around for years, so I didn't really think that was the reason. Boomer had gone away before for a couple of days here and there but he had always come back.

Throughout the first weeks of shooting my show I woke up every morning wondering if Boomer would reappear. Waking up was harder because Boomer was also my alarm clock: Every morning he would go into the crawl space under the house and let out his raspy meow just beneath my bedroom, asking me to feed him. After about a week I knew he probably wasn't coming back.

Boomer was a unique and very intuitive cat. He had a full range of emotions that you could read on his face. He had been a feral kitten when I got him at a shelter in 2002. A crazy antisocial cat that evolved into a warm, sweet guy. There were obstacles along the way. My second wife and I got him to keep another cat we had company. That was a female cat called Butch, who died young. I was away when she died. My ex said that Boomer really showed up for her after Butch. I'm glad someone did. I was away a lot. Boomer had that sense. He knew when you were hurting and he would be there for you.

Boomer had one flaw: He peed on everything. I mean everything. You never saw him do it. We thought about setting up cameras in the house to catch him but there was really no point, since he was the only cat. He peed in luggage, on shoes, on books, on furniture, where we made food, everywhere. It's amazing how much of that behavior cat people will tolerate before something forces them to take action. One of two things has to happen. Either friends come over and, immediately upon entering your home, say something along the lines of "Holy shit, did a giant cat pee on your house?" You respond with something along the lines of "Wow, really? I can't even smell it." Or you end up spending a good chunk of your day wandering around your house smelling general areas, trying to focus in on where the pee is, until one day you realize that what you are wearing is the source of the smell and you think, "How did he pee on me? We have to do something about this."

I remember the night of the discussion with my second wife, Mishna, because it offered a window into her soul that was jarring. We were lying in bed and I said, "What are we going to do about Boomer peeing on everything?" Without even a pause she said, "Let's just put him down." It was unsettling. I always knew she was a little cold-hearted, but that was disturbing. It also fed my paranoia on a cultural level. She came from German stock. As a Jew I thought that way of thinking was a slippery slope that probably led to the Final Solution. In retrospect that was probably a little extreme but you get my point.

We put Boomer outside to live. That was humane but hard for me. I worry. There were other cats out there. Mishna acquired a calico kitten to keep Boomer company. That was Moxie. Moxie was a fat, shameless, needy cat. She was very smart but she annoyed me. I like ferals. You have to earn their respect, and even then it's tentative. Boomer and Moxie became inseparable. When I split with my ex I made her take Moxie. I guess I wanted Boomer to feel heartbreak too. I don't think he ever forgave me for that.

After she left me I let Boomer back in at night because he understood my pain and carried me a bit. He was solid. Once too many things became marked with pee he was out again.

Jessica, who lives with me now, built a sweet relationship with Boomer. She would go out on the deck to smoke every day and hang out with him. When we broke up for a while she actually came back to the house when I wasn't there to spend time with Boomer. It was a little inappropriate but I get it now. I'm not sure whom she liked more, actually. He was just a deep cat. Now that he's gone she can't go out on the deck anymore. It's too sad for her.

Boomer and I went through a lot of shit together. Emotional upheavals, breakups, long periods of time apart, other cats coming and going, women coming and going, but he was always there, out on the deck, with his raspy voice and telling eyes.

I don't want this to be a downer. I want to dedicate this book to Boomer and to personal growth, to evolving.

Why he vanished just as my life was changing drastically demands interpretation. I am not religious or spiritual, but I am prone to connecting dots in equations so that they defy coincidence. Someone suggested that maybe this was the end of our journey together, that he had taken me as far as he could and that it was time for him to move on. I like that angle.

Throughout the shoot, beneath acting and showing up and whatever else the job entailed, was a profound sadness but an even more profound hope. When someone or something you love disappears or moves on, it feels negotiable. Maybe we'll get back together, maybe they'll come back, maybe they are in a better place for them and I have to accept that there are things out of my control. These are all difficult emotional options, especially the last one. If you are alive and awake, sadness is a fluctuating constant. Hope is fleeting, a decision you make out of faith, desire, or desperation. Cats know more than we can understand. I don't care about biology and brain size.

I don't think about what could've happened to him too much. The best-case scenario is that he wandered off and found some nice old lady with some sweet wet food and a warm house with no other cats in it to compete with him and he's living the life. Isn't that what we all want?

If I find that lady, I will thank her and take my cat back, even if he is happier there. I guess I'm selfish.

Acknowledgments

Thank you Jessica Sanchez for matching my crazy and loving me. Thanks Mom and Dad for eventually being okay with what is in this book. Thank you Brendan McDonald for cutting things right and keeping it steady. Thank you Amy Gottschalk for your focus and obsession. Thanks Olivia Wingate and Kelly Van Valkenburg for being the part of my brain that keeps things organized. Thanks Daniel Greenberg for getting the good deal. Thanks Chris Jackson and Laura Van der Veer. Holy shit, right? We made a book. Thanks to all the *WTF*ers of all kinds! Boomer lives!

Marc Maron is a stand-up comedian and host of the podcast *WTF with Marc Maron*. He has appeared in his own comedy specials on Comedy Central and HBO, and his sitcom *Maron* airs on IFC. He lives in Los Angeles.